A selection of reviews of Pottery Cottage

Available as a paperback or Kindle from Amazon

www.amazon.co.uk/Pottery-Cottage-crime-sbook-Britain/dp/1999702670

Alan is a master storyteller - David Mastin, newspaper executive

Detailed extremely well and a real page turner - Karen Smith

Brilliantly written - Amazon customer

Terrifyingly brilliant - Colin Sanders

A truly despicable crime but a captivating read - Amazon customer

Un-put-downable - Amazon customer

Plan to stay awake all night reading - Amazon customer

A must-have book for fans of the genre - Sarah Kenneally

Fantastically written with such care and consideration for the family - Vonnie

Brilliant informative novel based on a true story - Cormac McCarthy

Exceptional writing - Sandra Shanks

My best read this year - Micky E

You will not be disappointed - Mrs J A Hughes

Please read this book. Alan Hurndall writes so well - Amazon customer

Heartbreaking - I read it in two days - Lisa

Unforgettable - Miss Marple on Amazon

Masterful - a challenging, meticulous portrayal - M W Carey

Only read if you don't have other responsibilities! - Amazon customer

Truly a gem and a Truman Capote of our day - Alm

THE CROOKED SPIRE KILLINGS

"All looks yellow to the jaundiced eye"

Alexander Pope, quoted by defence QC Rudolph Lyons

ALAN HURNDALL is an award-winning journalist and film maker working in newspapers and television. He is a former Campaigning Journalist of the Year, a BAFTA nominee, and a Royal Television Society winner. He was a lecturer in journalism and media law at Sheffield Hallam University and holds a Master's Degree in Creative Writing. The Crooked Spire Killings is his third non-fiction book.

By the same author

The Invisible Girl

Pottery Cottage

First published 2022

ISBN No 978-1-8384926-0-1

Printed by Northend, Sheffield, England.

Front cover: Maddie Wright

The following is a true story of events that happened in England and Germany in the early 1960s. Characters are real, although in a few cases names have been changed to protect the identities of people who might still be alive. Dialogue is taken from learned journals, witness statements, court hearings, press reports, interviews by the author, and recollections of people from the time. Some dialogue has been imagined but based on conversations known to have taken place.

The author would especially like to thank the following

The Stobbs Family, especially Jerry and Georgina

Carole Adams

Tim Peacock

Tony and Angela Fry

Geoff A Robinson

Dirty Stop Outs Guide to 1960s Chesterfield

Destination Chesterfield

Chesterfield Black and White Tour

Matthew Crampton, author of The Trebor Story

Sarah Foden, Mondelez International

Dr Richard Shepherd, author of Unnatrual Causes

Peter Brooks, author of The Pretty Windows Murder

The British Medical Journal

The Police Journal

Phil Bramley, Derbyshire Times

The Sheffield Star

The News of the World

Birmingham Post

Journal of The Royal Society of Medicine

The Independent

The British Library

The Daily Mirror

English Heritage

The Morning Telegraph

Chesterfield Public Library

The Daily Herald

John Raine

Reflections Magazine

Sheffield City Library

Darren Williams

Linda Poppenborg

The Sunday Pictorial

The Guardian

PREFACE

The Sixties will forever stand in history as the decade of revolution - in sex equality, civil rights, fashion, music, race and social attitudes. But as a new decade dawned, and the Frumpy Fifties gave way to the Swinging Sixties, change was a long way off. Grey was yet to morph into rainbow psychedelia, hemlines were respectable, hair was short, zips were up, buttons fastened and bras yet to be burned. Conscription was only slowly being phased out, you could still be hanged by the State, and more than 400 years after it was first criminalised, it was still against the law for men to engage in homosexual activity.

The Buggery Act of 1533 outlawed sodomy throughout the British Empire, punishable by death. For centuries sodomy attracted a minimum of ten years imprisonment. In 1960 in Great Britain homosexuality was not only illegal, but regarded as an illness, a disease, a perversion. The term 'gay' still meant happy, carefree, bright. They were called bent, benders, homos, queers, poofters. Many men were shamed into electric shock treatment to 'straighten' their warped minds. This state-sanctioned homophobia ruined lives and destroyed reputations. Homosexual sex was unlawful, meaning that even acts in private could be prosecuted. A letter expressing terms of affection between two men was all that was required to bring about a prosecution. Just being in the wrong person's notebook could land a man in jail. It meant that no queer male could be 'out' - at work, at school, college, often to their families. They were gagged by society from talking about whom they met, whom they liked, whom they loved.

Most male relationships had to be secretive, liaisons confined to seedy places like public lavatories, dark alleyways, and isolated spots in the countryside. It was a shadowy, sinful existence. Homosexuals were derided and despised by the public, and blackmailed and bullied by the police, even though they were more often the victims of hate crimes than perpetrators. This prejudice resulted in bruised souls, battered bodies and shattered minds. Isolation. Mental illness. Depression. Suicide. And, in the small middle-England town of Chesterfield, murder…

PART ONE

WILLIAM ARTHUR ELLIOTT

Sheffield, England,
Sunday June 12th 1960

In his student digs near the city centre, Roland Ingram pored over
an Ordnance Survey map of the Peak District, a mug of instant coffee
steaming beside him. It was a warm but blustery morning, and he was
about to do what he loved best - take his bike out to the countryside.
And what better place to explore on a holiday weekend than Britain's
first national park, right on his doorstep?

He was already dressed in his cycling gear and had meticulously
planned a thirty mile or so round trip to one of Derbyshire's most
historic pubs, the 600-year-old Fox and Goose in the hamlet of Wigley.
He folded the map, grabbed his rucksack, and within five minutes was
unlocking his Raleigh in the ginnel ready to set off.

Sheffield was built around seven hills - a nightmare for cyclists. The
east was flatter, but with pollution and smoke from the steelworks,
factories and coalfields, it was an obvious no-go area. But out to
the west, there was fresh air and mile upon mile of rolling hills and
magnificent views. His route took him from the terraced streets to
where the houses became detached, stone replaced brick, and concrete
turned to grass. But on a long descent just after Owler Bar, a large rural
roundabout on the south-west outskirts of Sheffield, the wind got up
and he hit trouble - a 'blizzard' of dead vegetation. One moment he
was freewheeling in fresh air, the next forced to breathe through his
nose, with his head down, eyes half-closed, spitting out fragments of
moorland ash.

***

The contamination was the result of a meteorological fluke the
previous year. Then, Derbyshire had somehow dodged every major
thunderstorm that had blown in from north, east, south or west. Only
six inches of rain had fallen all year, making it the driest Spring and
Summer in those parts since records began in 1842. The hills and
the moors were tinder dry, just waiting for the spark. It came on the
first day of September and brought widespread destruction to one of
Britain's most beautiful landscapes. In eleven days, across a 40-mile
stretch of countryside between Penistone, north east of Sheffield, and
Matlock, to the south, there were at least 700 separate fires. Barlow East
Moor burned for ten days; Totley Moor for six; Beeley, Burbage and

Hathersage Moors, for four. Smoke and embers filled the landscape. Hundreds of fire crews and volunteers manned the moors day and night, fighting a lost cause. Then, on day twelve, relief. At last, the rains came and achieved what man couldn't do. When the clouds rolled away, the damage was there for all to see - ugly scars across thousands of acres of grassland, heather, and peat. When the peaks dried, and the breezes blew, it snowed ash. And anything dropped, dumped, or buried in those hills, verges and valleys, would soon be covered in a thin layer of black soot.

***

Roland swung a left near the bottom of the A621 onto a moorland road called Clod Hall Lane. He was about to stumble on something he could never have imagined or expected; something that would live in his memory - something that would trigger the biggest criminal investigation in the history of the Derbyshire Police Force.

On the blackened verge he could just make out the legs of a man. The body was next to a stone wall and partially hidden by fire debris. He left his bike on the road to investigate. He inched forward, a mixture of trepidation and intrigue. The man, whom he guessed was in his sixties, was lying face down. He was fully clothed, in a suit, but his shoes were missing. His arm was extended over his head and there was a small pool of dried blood under his forehead. It was clear he was dead. On the man's head, someone had arranged a pattern of grass, neat and artistic, like some sort of ritual marking. He looked around. The only building was a gamekeeper's lodge but there was no sign of anyone. He figured the nearest phone box would be in Baslow, two miles away. He remounted and cycled like the wind.

Clod Hall Lane where the body was found

-2-

Private Michael Copeland threw open the train door, tossed his kitbag out from the carriage, and leapt down onto the platform. Behind him the loco huffed and puffed as though it was getting its breath back after a long run in the sweltering heat.

It was the start of the Whitsun Holiday week. The temperature threatened to hit 80 later, and the train was packed with holidaymakers heading for the coast. Families with suitcases and buckets and spades jostled to board against the tide of disembarking passengers. Amid the chaos of hissing steam, the shrill of excited kids, porter shouts, platform whistles and slamming doors, he helped a young mother retrieve her pram from the guard's van and saluted back as she thanked him. The air was sticky and humid and filled with the familiar perfume from the sweet factory that towered above the station goods yard. He looked up at the skyline. The engine's smoke had evaporated to reveal a blue, cloudless sky. The famous crooked spire glinted in the sun. It felt good to be home again, even if he always couldn't wait to leave. Dressed in his civvies, no-one could have guessed he was a serving soldier. He was in great shape, over six feet tall, and bursting with muscle from years down the pit and working out in Army gyms. Even his face looked strong, with cheeks of stone and a 'Desperate Dan' jutting jaw that stretched down to his collar.

He joined the line of passengers waiting to have their tickets clipped - day-trippers; two young lads in colourful T shirts, shorts and sandals and carrying a cricket bat; women on a shopping expedition, their milky-white skin about to get its first exposure of the summer; teenagers, soon to get up to no good. A group of girls walked by and giggled as he checked them out. He handed over his travel warrant for inspection. Behind him the porter's whistle blew and amid another burst of steam, the train chugged away to its next destination.

The working-class town of Chesterfield stood on a massive coalfield in Britain's industrial heartland. It was served by rail and a canal to the River Trent, once a cheap transit to the east for the lead, iron and earthenware produced in the vicinity. Goods made here were found in millions of homes. Robinson's, producers of one of the first disposable nappies; Trebor, whose sweets were the thrill of every kid in the country; Dema, makers of most of the country's beer and wine glasses; and Donkin's, manufacturing valves and other components for the gas industry.

Chesterfield railway station, as depicted by Geoff Robinson

Like most of Britain, it had seen a steady rise in its standard of living. There was more job security, less stress in their lives, and Chesterfield folk were as friendly as anyone. The memories of war shortages and rationing were fading fast. The colour was back on faces and clothes. The first summer of the Sixties had dawned, and with 'coin' in their pockets and purses, it seemed everyone wanted to spend.

He'd been stuck in a stuffy carriage for three hours with five strangers, reading the paper, doodling, getting some shut eye, and through half-closed eyes, gawping at the pins of the woman opposite. He was gagging for a pint, but the pubs weren't open yet, so he queued for the phone.

Michael Copeland

3

In a cottage in a Chesterfield suburb, it was the usual Saturday morning routine for the Wakeford family. Dad was going through the week's figures from his insurance broker business, while in the kitchen, his wife drew up her shopping list and counted the Green Shield stamps in her voucher books. In her bedroom their only child Julie, 19, painted her nails. Just in case. The phone rang out from the table in the hall.

'I'll get it,' she said, rushing down the stairs to beat her parents to the receiver.

'Walton 6943. Julie speaking,' she answered.

'Ay up me duck.'

It took a moment for her to register the voice. There was an awkward silence, then… 'Thought you said you'd write,' she said loftily.

'I'm more a face-to-face person,' he replied.

She thought of making a crude joke but bit her lip. 'Where are you, anyhow?'

'I'm home. Two weeks leave. What you up to tonight?'

'Why do you ask?' she said, with a semblance of hard-to-get. He hadn't contacted her since they'd met on his last visit back at Christmas. That evening had ended in a drunken one-night stand. Even though she was a willing participant, she felt she'd been used.

'I was thinking of the Vic again,' he offered.

'Maybe. Depends. What time?'

'Eight. Meet you outside.'

'Do you even remember what I look like?'

'Don't get sarky. I'll be wearing a pink carnation and have a newspaper under my arm. See you later then. And, er… put your dancing shoes on!'

He rang off before she could reply. Her dad emerged from the dining room. 'Who was that?'

'An old friend… he's taking me out. I'll need a lift, though…'

'One day I'll say no. I'm not a bloody taxi.'

'Come on, dad. You know you want to.' She pecked him on the cheek and bounced upstairs to decide what to wear.

***

His date sorted, he swaggered up the hill to the town centre, a cocky, arrogant walk. He knew every inch of those cobbled streets and their funny names dating back hundreds of years. Places like The Shambles, Knifesmithgate, Glumangate, and Low Pavement; the maze of alleyways; one of the country's biggest markets; the Market Hall, with its iffy barber, and the putrid smells of raw meat and fish; and the grand clock tower, all grimy and black, with its distinctive clang. And then there were the pubs. He'd got bladdered in most over the years and scrapped in some - the Corner House, Gardener's Arms, Queen's Head, the Three Horseshoes, Commercial Inn, the notorious Crown and Cushion, the Punchbowl, the King and Miller, and the Royal Oak, the town's oldest ale house.

Copeland's 'manor' (Geoff Robinson)

As a kid, while his Mum and Dad supped inside, he'd sit on the stone steps drinking lemonade with a colouring book and crayons. He'd been a little bugger, if truth be known, running amok through the market stalls, knocking over displays of fruit, pilfering, and being chased by stallholders. When it rained, he'd played 'waterfalls' - poking a stick up

13

at the tarpaulins sending cascades of water over the sides, much to the anger of drenched shoppers. Now, at 22 and all grown up, he felt the town was his. He could do what he wanted.

He wandered into the Post Office and withdrew some spend from his Savings Account, flirting with the assistant who was explaining the ins and outs of sending a telegram abroad.

'Where to?' she asked.

'Verden an der Aller,' he said, dismissive and confident.

'Where's that?'

'Germany when I last looked,' he replied, this time with a twinkle in his eye.

He produced a crumpled-up piece of paper of fancy continental lettering and numbers of an address on a road called Borsteler Weg. 'It's my lass... I want to say I've arrived safe and I'm missing her and am looking forward to seeing her again soon.'

'Oh, how romantic!' she said, 'cost a bloody fortune, that.' She looked at him quizzically. 'First timer, eh! A telegram I mean.'

'Aye. A virgin, you could say.'

She told him that you had to pay for each letter, even the spaces. After much experimentation and crossing out he ended up with 'Ingrid. Homeok.MissUx,' the 'x' denoting a single kiss instead of the original three.

Outside, the smell of fish and chips and mushy peas drifted up from Boden's. But he'd promised himself a pork stuffing cob from Kirk's where, on market days, trays of sausage rolls came down on the pulley from heaven every 15 minutes. He wandered into a small backstreet tailor to collect his new suit. It was a pale green lightweight affair he'd bought off the peg for £9 in the Christmas sale, but needed to have altered. It had hung in a backroom ever since. In the sweaty little fitting room, he admired himself in the mirror and combed his hair for the umpteenth time that day. Slicked back - thanks to an obsession with Brylcream. A few doors along he bought a pair of grey leather slip-ons to match.

***

Soon after midday, Copeland found himself in the Spread Eagle, near the bus station, supping his first of the day. Some 'Trebba' girls - workers from the Trebor factory - were celebrating someone's birthday and were already well on the go, but he gave them a wide berth. Instead, he settled next to a group of half a dozen or so men playing dominoes, all the while 'tab 'anging,' listening to their private jokes and innuendos, while rolling his own from a tin of Golden Virginia. It took a while to cotton on that they were different, like some private club - middle-aged blokes with their secret slang, coded signals, whispered asides, knowing looks and private jokes, all looking like his fucking teachers with their shiny suits, wispy hair and thick-framed glasses. He took an instant dislike.

After an hour or so one got up to go - a little fellow in a suit, balding and bespectacled, looking like a professor. Copeland left his drink unfinished. Out of the door, down a little alleyway, he stalked him all the way, like a private eye in a movie. At the public toilets on Markham Road the man stopped. Copeland stood in a doorway and watched. The man waited outside for a while, urgently looking around as if expecting - or fearing - someone emerging from the crowd. After a couple of minutes, a much younger man, a builder perhaps, covered in plaster dust and wearing hob-nailed boots, shorts and a string vest, arrived and loitered a few yards from the entrance. The two didn't speak, just exchanged subliminal looks. They went inside a few seconds apart. Copeland took a drag of his roll up. Watching. Aroused. Angry.

I fucking knew it! Bum bandits. Rear gunners... perverts, the lot of 'em.

4

On the southern edge of town Harry Copeland was putting the finishing touches to his son's homecoming tea. He wanted the day to be special and had been out first thing buying the bits and pieces for 'our Micky's' feast. He'd fussed over the butcher as he carved ham off the bone, bought some continental cheese and Spam from the Co-op, tomato sausages from the Market Hall, and queued at the baker's for a huge loaf of crusty white bread - none of that Mother's Pride sliced rubbish. On the way home he dropped by the 'offy' for some beers. For afters, Mrs Heath, his 'housekeeper,' had baked an apple pie and left heating instructions. All he had to do was put the oven on and make the Bird's packet custard.

Harry had lived in the same redbrick semi on the St Augustines estate for virtually all his married life. He and wife Rosie moved there shortly after their first child Michael was born, in 1939 when the development was new, and they raised their four boys there.

St Augustine's Crescent

It was convenient for town - just a mile away - with a decent garden for Harry's new hobby of growing spuds. It was the kind of community where everyone knew everyone. They sat on the step and chatted over a brew or a bottle - some even moved a settee into the front garden.

You could leave your door unlocked, and folk looked out for each other. When Michael was born, the hospital phoned a neighbour - one of the few in the street to have a phone - to break the news that Harry was now the father of a bonny lad.

He grew up to be a sinner and a saint. Good at art, creative, but loved a scrap too. In his teens he got into trouble with the law for petty theft and received borstal training. But Harry stood by his son whatever. Michael had gone to Spire Juniors around the corner, and on to the local secondary modern. Two-thirds of the boys there left school at 15, consigned to a life of manual labour down the pit, in the steelworks or in factories. And so, still only a kid in everyone's eyes except the law, their lad became a miner, doing light duties at Markham Colliery at Staveley five miles away. For adult men it was hot, dirty and dangerous. Indeed, in the month their boy was born, 79 miners were killed there when tubs carrying coal ran out of control and collided with an electric joint box. The sparks ignited coal dust and sent a wall of fire through the seam where the men were working. The year before that, nine men had been killed in a similar accident.

Rose died young - aged 46 - when Michael was 17, and they grieved together. The lad went off the rails. He went on a burglary spree and was caught breaking into a shop in Wingerworth with a shotgun which he fired into the ceiling. He was sent to Huntercombe Borstal in Nuffield, Oxfordshire but escaped and went on the run, stealing at least three cars, and sleeping rough. He ended up in the West Country, holed out in a barn at Winchcombe, in Gloucestershire. He was only caught after he broke into the farmhouse while the female occupant was sleeping and stole food, drink and possessions.

Harry always had difficulty understanding the ways of his boy. One minute kind and caring, the next in some kind of trouble or other. He fed birds in his room and once brought home an injured rabbit cradled in his arms and cried when it had to be put down. That night he'd got smashed, and involved in yet another punch-up. But now the Army seemed to have sorted him out, made a man of him.

So, with the feast prepared, when Harry heard that distinctive rat-a-tat-tat on the door, his heart missed a beat - mostly in anticipation but with a degree of trepidation.

'Nah then youth,' said Harry, his normal greeting to anyone aged ten and upwards. They hugged on the doorstep… a long continuous hold which said far more than words or kisses could ever convey.

'How was your journey?'

'Couldn't wait. Bloody parched.'

'I hope you haven't eaten…'

Over the meal they talked about Harry's job as a labourer. They both thought he was getting a bit old to be lumping bricks and bags of cement. And then Germany. 'How is it over there?' asked Harold.

'Yeah, loving it to be fair. Oh, that reminds me. I bought you a present.' He handed his father a flick knife, with a long blade, one side serrated.

'I bought it near the barracks. Got two. One for myself.'

Harry looked at his son proudly. 'I knew the Army would be the making of thee. Mum would've been pleased you've finally settled down.'

'Did I tell ya I've got a girlfriend?'

'You never have…'

'German lass, works at the camp telephone exchange. Speaks effing good English, mind. It's all a bit hush-hush… let's just say that neither the Army nor her parents approve.'

'How often d'ya see her?'

'Every night, virtually.'

'What, they let you out every night?'

He mocked a German accent.

'Nein… but I 'ave vays and meanz…'

Harry chuckled. That's my lad.

5

'Pogged out,' he napped on the sofa in the middle of Grandstand. It had been a long and somewhat emotional day.

He ran a bath then put on his new outfit, meticulously folding a tie in his pocket to get past the bouncers on the door. As the heat died, he wandered up to town. It took about 20 minutes, the scenic route, along Park Road beside Queen's Park. Harry stayed in, watching an old British spy movie called Knight Without Armour, starring Marlene Dietrich. The Cold War had dominated the headlines for years. Earlier the TV news had reported on tensions between Russia and America as the two rival presidents, Krushchev and Eisenhower, traded insults over the future of Germany. His son was in the heart of it all, he thought, holding the Superpowers at bay.

In town, the alleyways and cobbled streets were awash with people - groups of lads and lasses, courting couples, white collar workers, factory employees, mods, rockers, beatniks, students, and miners from the surrounding pit villages, scrubbed up to take wives and girlfriends for a night out. The three picture houses - the Regal, Gaumont and Odeon - all had long queues. The pubs were already busy. Laughter, chat, jukeboxes, live music, rowdy singalongs, rang out.

Shortly before 8pm, he arrived at the Victoria Ballroom. The 'Vic' stood in the shadow of the crooked spire, behind a black and white mock-Tudor façade modelled in the 1920s on Chester. It had been the town's main dancing venue for thirty odd years, responsible for thousands of romances and an equal number of broken hearts.

He could see Julie waiting anxiously in a doorway opposite, a tall slim figure with long dark hair. He studied her for a few seconds before showing his face. She certainly looked grand - a ballgown, white bobby socks and ballerina-style flat shoes. She wore thick red lipstick and a pair of cotton gloves. He pecked her on the cheek and held her hand. She could smell stale beer on his breath but said nothing. 'Oh, before I forget,' he said. He reached inside his jacket pocket and produced a white postcard with a drawing on one side. On the back it read, 'To Julie, sorry for not keeping in touch.' She couldn't believe the detail. There was no outline, just sweeps of charcoal of different shades and directions colliding and forming an image of a squirrel holding a nut.

'This is brill. Did you draw this?'

'Bored on the train,' he shrugged with a smile.

He suggested they go for a drink in the King and Miller opposite the ballroom. But she wanted to go straight in, so they joined the queue outside the huge glass doors. The mood inside was friendly and convivial. They went to the bar and he bought a pint of bitter for himself and a cider for her.

The Alf Needham Big Band, dressed in tuxedos and bow ties, was in full swing. After the live music, it was disco time. The suits and frocks stepped aside to allow the teddy boys and girls to strut their stuff. It was a colourful sight - drape jackets, velvet collars, drainpipe trousers, and pencil skirts, ducktails and slicked-back hairdos, jiving and rocking and rolling, and even doing the twist, the new dance craze from America. Sipping their drinks, the couple had little to say. He seemed distant and distracted, not bothering to engage beyond one-word answers.

'You okay?' she shouted above the music.

'Yeah. Why do you ask?'

'You seem a bit quiet, that's all.'

'I'm knackered to be fair.' Truth was, his thoughts were dominated by those dirty bastards he saw earlier in the pub.

As the lights dimmed, she practically had to drag him to the dance floor. They swooned to the number one, Cathy's Clown, a close-harmony guitar lament by the Everly Brothers. She held him tight and moved closer to dance cheek to cheek. He could smell her scent and she could feel him. But he began to get those thoughts again. It was happening more and more of late. Arousal often triggered revulsion, rage even. And instead of showing tenderness, he suddenly wanted to throttle her.

'I need a drink,' he said and stomped off, leaving her on the dancefloor, surprised, stranded and embarrassed. She ran off in tears and he watched her disappear into the throng of revellers. Spoilt bitch. He retired to the bar. She was already on her way to the bus station. Going home. Alone. The date had lasted precisely 90 minutes.

He supped his pint and wandered back out into the sultry night... under the crooked spire, down the alleyways onto Beetwell Street, past the nick... and into the Spread Eagle. Would they still be there?

Chesterfield at night

Montages by Geoff Robinson

-6-

Two hours or so later - shortly before midnight, in fact - Ted Winfield was collecting glasses and clearing-up ready to retire for the night. He was the landlord of the Boythorpe Inn, near Queen's Park, a mile or so out from the town centre, and on Copeland's route home.

If the factories were the lifeblood of the local economy, then the park was its lungs, a welcome expanse of green in the heart of a grey industrial landscape. Pollution and overcrowding had always dogged the town. In 1887 Chesterfield's forefathers decided the locals needed relief and purchased acres of land to mark Queen Victoria's Golden Jubilee. They later added a bandstand, boating lake, cycling track and cricket pitch, and planted specimen trees - lime, oak, holly horse chestnut - around the perimeter. However, at night, the park's barren annexe in particular was also the scene of what locals described as 'goings on.' And Ted's pub was opposite the annexe gates.

He heard voices outside, then someone banging on the door. On the pavement were three men and a girl helping a man who was bleeding and groggy.

'We need your help. This man's been badly beaten up.' Ted beckoned them in and sat the victim down.

'I'll get something,' he said, retreating behind the bar. He returned with a tea towel and a bowl of warm water. The girl bathed the poor man's wounds. There was blood and mud on his face. His jaw was the shape of a rugby ball and almost certainly fractured.

'What happened?' asked Ted.

The man was reluctant to go into detail except that he was wandering home through the park annexe and was attacked by a 'soldier type' and punched and kicked to the head. 'Do you want me to phone the police?' said Ted.

'No... I'll be fine.'

Ted knew the score. The annexe was a known haunt of late-night homosexual activity. There had been repeated cases over the years of men being assaulted by 'queer bashers.' But the victims never pressed charges.

'What's your name, mate?'

'Not important,' he said, shaking his head.

'Well, you need to get that looked at. I'll drop you at Casualty.' The man with no name nodded.

-7-

The next day

Julie spent Sunday moping around the house feeling sorry for herself and turning over events in her mind. Had she been too hasty storming out of the ballroom? Then, mid-afternoon, when she was alone, the phone went. It was him.

'I'm sorry,' he grovelled. 'I don't know what got into me.' He'd looked everywhere for her and realised what a fool he'd been, allowing her to rush home alone. She listened without reply, knowing that if she said anything she would probably cry.

He persisted. 'Look, I really like you and I want to make it up to you. I've grown very fond of you. Will you come out with me tomorrow night? We'll go for a walk and I can apologise in person,' he pleaded. She thought for a second. It was no good.

'I'm sorry, but... I just can't,' she blurted. 'Thanks for the squirrel.' There seemed nothing more to say and she put the receiver down.

In the afternoon he took a bus to The Peak District. His favourite spot was Curbar Edge, a seven-mile ridge of undulating ground overlooking the beautiful Derwent Valley. This was his bolt hole, a sanctuary away from trouble in his life and troublesome thoughts in his head, where he would lose himself for hours, sketching, painting and writing poems, using the splendour of the views as inspiration for his art. He called it meditating.

His room at home was adorned with his pastel and charcoal creations of Peak views and wildlife, often portraying feelings of loneliness, a bleakness of mind, and a barren emptiness. He stripped down to his waist and sat on the rocks watching the birds hover and dive in the thermal currents. He lay back on his rucksack, closed his eyes and enjoyed the tranquillity, interrupted only by the rustle of the breeze and the twitter of the birds. He'd been back only a day and already there was so much going through his head. He decided to head back home, hit town later and get pissed, as he would virtually every day for the rest of his leave.

Curbar Edge, the Peak District

Copeland's charcoal creations

-8-

That Saturday

Chesterfield Market dated back hundreds of years to when Lords and Ladies in their finery mingled with labourers from the fields and factories, arriving in carriages and on foot to seek local produce - corn, cattle, silk, hats and lace.

This day, it was mostly women in cotton dresses, men in jeans, and youths in shorts and basketball vests. Copeland spent Saturday afternoon ducking among the stalls and in and out of pubs looking... well, he didn't really know for what.

Somewhere in the crowd, pottering about and browsing the second-hand books, was former Home Guard Bill Elliott. He lived in the picturesque Peak District town of Bakewell, where the River Wye wound its way around green fields and woodlands, flowed past rows of mellow stone houses, and under the medieval five-arched bridge. He was a polite, private man - balding and bespectacled - who worked as a nine-till-five clerk in a college. He was a creature of habit. He simply loved Saturdays. It was his chance to be anonymous in the wider and wilder world of Chesterfield, half an hour away. There he would enjoy a few shandies in The Spread Eagle or The Three Horse Shoes and seek out male company. He was a formal individual, who felt out of place in casual attire. He dressed smartly for the outings, although today was warm and for once he regretted wearing a suit.

Bakewell, where William Elliott lived

People in Bakewell knew him not just for who he was, but more for the vehicle he drove - a quirky little 'bubble car.' Its bulbous headlights gave it the appearance of a cartoon character and kids used to wave as it ticked by. For years he roared about town on a motor bike, but then swopped it for the three-wheel Italian-designed Isetta, one of the smallest microcars on the road. He was nearing retirement and the 300cc engine achieved almost 100 miles to the gallon. What's more, he only needed a motorcycle licence to drive it. It was cheap to buy, economical to run, and at just 7ft long, and 4ft high, able to squeeze into the tiniest parking space. The car opened from the front, but Bill was a diminutive man - a lean 5ft 7ins - who could easily fit into the confined driving space. Critics dismissed them as 'death traps.' They were about to be proved right - but not in a way that any of them could ever have imagined.

The next morning

Fred Clarke lived in a small detached house on Park Road, Chesterfield, opposite Queen's Park. It was a delightful spot. Derbyshire played half their cricket matches there and in his garden in summer he often heard the 'thwack' of leather on willow and the ripple of polite applause drifting over the park perimeters.

But it was a far more dramatic sound that woke him in the middle of the night - a loud CRASH which he would later describe as a small explosion. This was followed by complete silence - 'no footsteps, no moans… nothing.' He sprang out of bed and looked out of the window. A bubble car had overturned on the road having obviously collided with a lamppost.

He rushed out fearing that the driver might be trapped inside. The vehicle was smashed and twisted. Its lights were off. The engine had stopped running but was contracting gently. The road was covered in debris - fragments of glass, a pair of horn-rimmed spectacles, a quantity of boiled sweets, and a lower set of dentures. What Fred thought must have been petrol flowed from the wreckage and down along the gutter, but strangely it smelt more like vinegar. In fact, it would transpire that a bottle of Sarson's malt had exploded. He dropped to his haunches to see if anyone was inside. Empty.

The street was deserted and lights came on. A neighbour, Len Robinson, appeared in his dressing gown. 'What's happened, Fred?'

'Call the police,' he shouted back.

The 999 call was routed through to Chesterfield Police headquarters in Beetwell Street, a few minutes away. It was 3am. In the canteen two constables, Wilf Howe and Roger Johnston, were enjoying a cuppa and writing up their reports of their earlier duties. Within a minute they were back in their Panda.

The crashed bubble car in Park Road

They arrived exactly ten minutes after the initial call. Just like Fred Clarke had done, their first task was to establish that no-one was trapped inside. The door was jammed but the officers managed to prise it open. Their torches picked out fresh bloodstains on the tartan upholstery and on a Mackintosh in the back. Bizarrely, a pair of shoes, with the laces tied, was wedged on the floor of the driver's seat 'as if someone had stepped out of them,' Howe would write in his report. What appeared to be bracken littered the seats and floor. They found a tin of rouge and a jar of Vaseline on the back seat. There were splashes of blood on the head lining behind the driver's seat and another larger blood stain in the centre of the seat. There were also blood stains outside the vehicle - around the smashed window and on the window frame.

By now, a crowd had encircled the stricken car, several in their nightclothes. 'Everyone. Please stand back and under no circumstances come near or touch the car or any of the debris in the road. Thank you,' shouted Johnston.

Howe radioed back to headquarters. 'Bizarre this one Guv. There's no sign of a driver, yet the door was jammed, so how did he get out?' They theorised that the driver could have been dazed and wandered off, although the question still remained about his exit. Maybe he'd been helped out by his passenger. A second patrol car cruised the area, making enquiries at Walton Hospital in case the driver was receiving treatment.

Howe began taking measurements of the scene while Johnston questioned the onlookers on what they'd seen or heard. Apart from the sound of the crash, the answer was nothing. Door to door seemed pointless. Everyone had been asleep.

At HQ they put in a request with the licensing authority for details of the owner. These would be back by daylight. The duty sergeant rang Chesterfield's Royal Hospital and enquired if anyone had been admitted with cuts and bruises in the last hour or so. He drew a blank. He decided there was little else they could do until daylight. One for CID maybe in the morning. He instructed the constables to protect the site until the scenes of crime people could attend later, and then the car would be taken to the police yard at Beetwell Street for forensic examination.

The crumpled bubble car

Leaving his partner to guard the wreckage, Johnston carried out a cursory search of the grounds and neighbouring annexe by torchlight, but with the moon hiding behind cloud, it was impossible to see beyond the range of the beam. The constables erected POLICE. SLOW signs and retired to their Panda, parked to protect the site from any early morning traffic. They began making notes.

'A rum do this my dear Watson!' joked Howe, 'a complete and utter mystery.'

They speculated what sort of person drove those weird machines.

'I don't know what to make of it,' said Howe, despite having seen pretty much everything in his fifteen years in the force. He reckoned it could have been the work of a joyrider who had run out of either control or petrol. He might have somehow got out and deliberately run the vehicle down the hill to crash it. 'Either that, or chummy was pissed and didn't want to get done for drink-driving so he legged it,' he said.

Johnston, who'd only been out of training six months, said, 'The make-up's a clue. Means it was driven by a woman, or at least a woman had been a passenger.'

'Or a man,' replied Howe.

'You what?'

'Rouge and lube? Don't be naïve, son. Didn't your mum tell you the facts of life?' Johnston contorted his face.

'That's disgusting,' he said.

Howe replied, 'Well, let's just write down what we know and leave it to the powers-that-be.'

Around dawn, the teleprinter at Chesterfield police station burst into life. It was the local vehicle tax authority forwarding the ownership details of an Isetta bubble car reg 488 KNU. It was registered to William Arthur Elliott, aged 60, with an address in Bakewell, 13 miles away.

The duty constable at Bakewell was alerted to check out if Elliott was at home. 'If not, find out as much as you can about him,' was the instruction. WPC Susan Thomas parked in a side road and walked up the drive of the well-kept stone semi. Freshly watered hanging baskets adorned the entrance and dripped onto the entrance. A woman in her late sixties opened the door. She was taken aback to find the police on her doorstep at nine o'clock on a Sunday morning.

'Hello. Sorry to disturb you. I'm WPC Thomas from just up the road at Bakewell police station. I'm looking for a Mr William Elliott. Is he in?'

'I've no idea. I haven't seen him this morning. I'd have to check his room.'

'Are you Mrs Elliott?'

'No, I'm Sarah, his sister. What's he done wrong?'

At that point an older woman appeared from the kitchen wiping her hands on a tea towel. 'What's going on?' she asked.

'They want to speak to Bill. But he's not up yet,' said Sarah. Turning to the officer she said 'This is my sister Martha. We all live here together.'

'You mind if I come in?' said the constable, one foot already in the door. She waited in the hall while they checked their brother's upstairs room. It didn't take long.

'Nope, he's not here. Not been slept in either by the looks of it. It's not unusual, though, is it Martha? He often stays out on a Saturday. You still haven't told me why you want to speak to him.'

'What car does he own?'

'It's one of those funny ones... you know, three wheels. Why do you ask?'

Thomas explained how the vehicle had been found crashed in Chesterfield with no sign of the driver. The sisters went pale. 'Is he all right?'

'Well, that's the point. There was no-one inside and we're trying to get to the bottom of why,' said the WPC. 'I take it you're both the next of kin.' The sisters nodded. There was a moment's silence.

'There's no need to worry at this stage. We've checked all the hospitals and there's no record of your brother being admitted or needing treatment. The car could have been stolen of course... or he ran out of petrol. It could be that he's stayed with a friend. That's why we want to contact him... to make sure he's come to no harm. You need to tell me the last time you saw him... and I'll need a list of acquaintances.'

The sisters looked at each other. 'He's a very private man. He doesn't discuss the people he meets when he's out,' said Martha.

'There was that one time a few years back,' interrupted Sarah, 'when he brought home that young man called John. He could only have been 24 or 25. He worked at H. Samuel, the jewellers in Chesterfield.'

Martha continued. 'He left here after breakfast saying he was going to the market in Chesterfield as usual and wouldn't be back until late. He often stays out late. He does his own thing,' she said.

'What about women? Is he going out with anyone?'

The sisters looked at each other. 'No, nothing like that. He's always preferred the company of men.'

'What about work mates or colleagues: could he be working today for instance?'

'No... he works Monday to Friday. It's a teacher training college so it's more a female environment.' The officer scribbled down a phone number.

'I'd be grateful for a call when he comes home or if you hear anything. I'll do the same if you could give me your number.'

With concern mounting over Elliott's disappearance, a 'post mortem' was carried out on the wreckage of his bubble car now parked in the yard at Beetwell Street police station. It was conducted by Jones and Cundy of the East Midlands Science Laboratory based in Nottingham. They were joined by Derbyshire CID officers examining for fingerprints.

Inside the crashed car

The forensic officers removed the door and recovered the pair of male shoes and the blood-stained Burberry raincoat. They also found a rolled-up plastic 'pack-a-mac' under the seat. All the contents, along with the spectacles and dentures found in the road, were photographed both on film and Polaroid, and collated for scientific examination. The seats were heavily stained with blood, and samples were cut out for lab tests. They retrieved branches of bracken from the floor but could not extract any meaningful fingerprints from anywhere.

The handbrake had not been applied and the gears were in neutral. The pipe leading to the carburettor was disconnected but the inspectors were divided as to whether or not the petrol pipe had been detached in the crash or deliberately snapped off. The main petrol tank was empty and although the reserve tank did contain petrol, the lever to supply the main tank was in the 'off' position. They speculated that if the main tank had run out of petrol it could have meant that the driver was hoping to travel further afield. If not, it was more likely that he lived nearby.

It was obvious that a person suffering from serious wounds had been carried in that car, but enquiries at hospitals failed to disclose anyone of Elliott's description having been brought in. He had completely vanished and his disappearance, coupled with his crashed car, provided a mystery - one that was about to become a lot clearer.

The next day

Murders were a rarity in this part of the world. And so was a call to Detective Inspector Ernest Bradshaw on a Sunday. He was about to tuck into a chicken salad with his family when the phone rang, alerting him to what looked like a killing in the Derbyshire countryside. A cyclist had stumbled across the body of a man on the roadside.

Bradshaw, a tall, thick-set man, was the son of a Sheffield postman, and had been in the police force for a quarter of a century - in CID for five. Three years previously he'd been awarded Police Long Service and Good Conduct medals. Now, approaching 50, he was one of Derbyshire's most senior detectives. He lived at Halfway, a village appropriately named given that it was roughly midway between Sheffield and Chesterfield. It took him 40 minutes speeding through the suburbs to arrive at the scene, receiving updates on his police radio on the way.

Clod Hall Lane was a long, isolated moorland road seven miles from Chesterfield. It was built by the Romans – mostly dead straight, but undulating to ride the contours of the land. His uniformed colleagues had already sealed off the road and protected the immediate area - roughly 200 yards from the main Baslow to Sheffield road - with tape. A line of various police vehicles was parked up and a handful of cadets were about to search the vicinity for clues, hampered by the fire soot. Roland Ingram, the student cyclist who found the body, was leaning against a stone wall, giving a statement to a constable. A police photographer was busy snapping the body and immediate surrounds.

Where the body was found

Turning into the road was Dr David Price, the duty Home Office
pathologist, and a consultant at the Beckett Hospital 35 miles away
in Barnsley. He was an expert in his field. Three years previously his
dogged skills had helped convict a man in the first documented case of
murder by insulin.

***

He'd been called to the Bradford home of Elizabeth and Kenneth
Barlow after Mr Barlow reported that he'd found his wife dead in a bath
full of water. At first glance, police assumed she'd drowned. However,
Price wasn't so sure, figuring it was rare for a 32-year-old adult to
drown in a domestic bath. He'd also noticed that a small cupful of water
remained in the cavity where the crook of her arm abutted the side of
the bath. This made her husband's story that he'd tried to resuscitate her
difficult to accept.

Barlow said his wife, who was pregnant, had taken a bath to cool
down because she was feeling hot. Indeed, police found her sweat-
drenched pyjamas in the house which supported that claim. But they
also discovered a couple of used syringes in the kitchen, but no sign
of any injectable medications. After a long post mortem, Price became
convinced she'd been rendered unconscious before she drowned and,
because of her excessive sweating and dilated pupils before death,
considered the possibility she'd been injected with insulin - at that time

the perfect murder weapon because it was undetectable after death.

His hunch troubled him and four days later he conducted a further examination of Mrs Barlow's body under spotlights and a magnifying glass. This revealed two miniscule hypodermic injection sites – one on each of her buttocks. He removed the tissue and with the help of a scientist from Boots, who'd been testing insulin absorption on rats and mice, Price was able to show she'd been injected with enough insulin to render her unconscious. Given that his wife was not diabetic, nor had she been prescribed the drug, the jury believed the prosecution case that since she couldn't possibly have injected herself, her husband must have killed her and they duly found him guilty of murder.

***

There was no need for such ground-breaking pathology here. The body of a man on a remote road, battered about the head, seemed an obvious case of murder but one thing he had learned in his career was never to presume. Everything had to be investigated no matter how clear-cut it seemed. He took off his jacket, rolled up his sleeves, and put his green apron on to set about his business in the June sunshine.

Bradshaw watched and waited, hoping for any scintilla of information that might kickstart his hunt for the killer. Like all murder cops he needed information fast. The most obvious was the man's identity and how and when he died.

Body temperature and rigor mortis were the best forensic indicators of the time of death but not always the most reliable. A hot body cooled, particularly if it had been left in the open countryside. The speed of rigor mortis was determined by temperature. Generally, the body would feel cold to touch within eight hours of death and rigor mortis could be established within three hours, but a body left outside in the open air could have no rigor after a week.

Price bent down and felt the man's body with the palm of his hand. It was cold. Rigor developed uniformly throughout the body but was most detectable in the small areas around the jaw, eyes and fingers, and these muscles were tight, although not completely stiff. He decided against taking a rectal temperature because of the man's clothing. That would be taken later at the lab. He also didn't want to risk contaminating the clothing.

'What do you make of this, Inspector?' Price asked the DI. He was referring to the pattern of loose grass arranged over the man's head and neck. Although the breeze had disrupted its design, it was artistic and definitely not scattered vegetation.

'Bizarre. It's almost ritualistic,' said Bradshaw. He asked the photographer to take a shot.

Price rolled the body on its side so he could see underneath. There was a small amount of congealed blood where his head had been. He allowed the corpse to roll back to its original position.

As the photographer worked around him, he made notes for his post mortem report, describing the scene and what he'd found. He then sketched a small diagram, especially noting the position of the bloodstains, the deceased's clothes and the precise position of the body. Bradshaw was sympathetic to the pathologist but his patience was wearing thin.

'What do you think, Doc?'

'I want to take him back for a PM as soon as... but as a rough guide I'd say he died between eight and 12 hours ago.'

'Oh, so quite recently then...'

'Hours rather than days, I'd say. I should know more by tonight,' said Price.

Bradshaw sighed and returned to his car. In the silence of his vehicle he contemplated what had happened. A car had crashed miles away, the owner was missing, and now a body had been found in the countryside. It was almost certain they were connected but he had to be sure. He rang Bakewell nick and ordered the local constable, WPC Thomas, who'd interviewed Elliott's sisters earlier, to meet him at the house in half an hour. In his pocket was a black and white Polaroid of the dead man's face, framed to show no apparent sign of assault except for black around the closed eyes. He could almost have been sleeping. Bradshaw also arranged for the Polaroids of exhibits found in the car to be ferried to Bakewell immediately. He asked the duty sergeant at Chesterfield to alert the media to a breaking story although not to give out details just yet. And to warn the brass they had a murder on their hands.

Bradshaw met up with Thomas outside Elliott's house. It was a distressing experience for all concerned, the sisters nodding grimly when shown the photographs. Yes, that was their brother, yes, those were his glasses, yes that was his mackintosh. It was only then that Bradshaw broke the news... their loved one had been found in the Peak District. And it was almost certainly the result of foul play.

Bradshaw assured the sisters that police would do all they could to find the person responsible. He had to get back, he said, but meanwhile could they tell his colleague everything they knew about their dead brother's movements and personal history.

Thomas put the kettle on and opened her notebook. Over cups of tea and through tears of grief, the women recalled how their brother was a quiet, generous and sweet man. They'd all lived in Bakewell for two years having grown up in rural Derbyshire, in the nearby village of Longstone, two miles away.

He'd worked at the nearby Thornbridge Estate since leaving school 40 years previously and was a trusted worker. He'd risen to become personal secretary to the estate owner Charles Boot, a Sheffield industrialist, Justice of the Peace, and the creator of Pinewood Studios. Bill had an intimate knowledge of the Hall and the Estate - so much so, that when Sheffield Corporation took it over to set up a teacher training college, they kept him on as a clerk. At one time they'd lived in the estate cottages but later moved to a house at beautiful Monsal Head which the sisters ran as a guest house.

They said Bill had taken little interest in local affairs, though during the War he'd served with the National Guard, protecting the Derbyshire countryside from possible invaders. His principal interest was motor-cycling and he'd only swapped his bike for the ill-fated three-wheeler car a year previously.

***

Even as they spoke, less than a mile away, at the site of a former workhouse, their brother was laid out on a mortician's slab at Newholme Hospital. The post mortem was the part of the job that Price loved - pure pathology detective work. He'd learned to detach any emotional feelings he had for the victim. The best he could do for him now was to use his professional skills to find the person responsible.

He had a legal duty to determine the cause, the formal part of his report that would appear on the death certificate. His first task was to exclude any chance that the victim had died naturally, then how quickly, and to make comment about possible weapons or events or actions that led to his injuries.

In his surgical plastic gloves and wearing a mask, Price began to remove the clothing, carefully placing each garment into a separate evidence bag for later forensic tests. He held the suit jacket up to the light. He could clearly see blood stains. He did the same with the trousers - there were grass marks and fragments of what appeared to be gravel. The man was shoeless, but his socks were clean of any mud or debris, immediately suggesting that he'd most likely been dumped rather than having met his death there. On his wrist was an expensive looking watch. After stripping the body, Price took swabs from the mouth and anus. These might give detectives clues to the circumstances leading up to his death, particularly if any sexual activity had taken place. He then took samples of the man's hair and clippings from his nails. These would later be analysed for skin or fibres or any other kind of debris that might offer clues linking him to the assailant or place. Other samples included blood, urine and human tissue for histology. Every exhibit was marked and numbered for Price's official report to the police and the coroner.

Bradshaw arrived from his meeting with the bereaved sisters. It was normal for senior officers to attend such an event - the crucial first stage of any murder investigation. Price offered him a drop of the brandy that he kept in a drawer for these occasions, but Bradshaw said he preferred a cuppa.

'We've got a formal ID,' Bradshaw said. 'William Elliott, aged 60. Lives just up the road.'

Price made the sign of the cross.

'Poor bugger. May he rest in peace.' And then he reached for his scalpel.

***

In that next hour or so, Price found 28 marks of recent violence about the head and body. The hyoid bone, the U-shaped bone at the root of the tongue in the front of the neck, was shattered. Both horns were broken and splayed outwards. 'It takes a lot to do that. I reckon whoever

41

did this stamped on his head repeatedly,' said Price.

He began dictating into his recording machine. The findings would be written up by a medical secretary first thing tomorrow morning.

'I found the body to be of a man, 5ft 7in tall, well-built and perfectly healthy. I have divided the injuries into four main groups. First, there were horseshoe marks and bruising behind the left ear and an interrupted line of marks across the front of the neck. They might be described as a series of dashes.

'Beneath the injury behind the ear was a horseshoe-shaped depressed fracture and the bone was broken in several places. Very great violence indeed would be required. The most likely instrument to cause these would be a boot or a shoe.

'The second group of injuries take the form of geometrical patterns of bruising on the right side of the face together with small cuts. These could have been caused when the head rested on a hard surface which had geometrical areas, together with limestone chippings, of which there are a great quantity on many roads at this time. The marks would arise out of the anvil effect if the head was lying on such a surface and stamped upon from the other side.

'The third group of injuries were marks of violence to the face, causing black eyes and could have been caused by a blow from a fist. The remaining group included many trivial marks of violence which could have been caused by a brawl or by a fall. My opinion is that death occurred between 8pm on June 11 and 2am on June 12. The cause of death was shock and inter-cranial haemorrhage following and due to fracture of the skull.'

Price switched off the machine and looked at Bradshaw. 'The absence of any significant amount of blood at the scene leaves me in little doubt that the murder was committed in some place other than where the body was found.'

'We found rouge and Vaseline in the car. Any evidence to suggest he was homosexual?'

'Not that I can tell, no.'

Bradshaw took stock. The tyre marks on the verge were consistent with a three-wheeler and the bracken in the car was similar to that growing in Clod Hall Lane. 'Taking your timings into account, I'm now convinced that the murderer, after dumping the body, drove the car to Park Road and abandoned it.'

Price interrupted. 'Oh, and one last thing. The condemned man's last meal... meat pie, peas and something containing currants, consumed a few hours before he died.'

13

Concern over the murder spread swiftly up the ranks of the
Derbyshire County Force. They urgently needed to know where the
killing took place and more about the victim's movements on that
Saturday.

One thing was certain. Without the public's help the investigation
could make little progress. A high-level news conference was arranged,
including the nationals. Britain had probably more national papers
than anywhere in the world, selling millions of copies every day. The
Daily Mirror, the working man's bible, alone sold several million. The
Press obviously loved a murder mystery and this was certainly worthy
of national coverage. A man found brutally battered in a National Park.
His car found abandoned in a town nearby. They quickly dubbed it the
'bubble-car murder.'

The police rolled out the top brass for the media briefing led by Det
Supt Stratton, head of Derbyshire CID. They handed out a photo of Mr
Elliott and asked the public if they saw him at any time on Saturday
or during the early hours of Sunday. Had anyone seen the distinctive
bubble car in that same period? 'We are appealing to the public, the
motorist, the late homegoer, the person going to work early on Sunday
- anyone who was on Clod Hall Lane or around Chesterfield who saw
anything or anyone. Particularly we would like to know if anyone was
asked for a lift, or saw a hitchhiker that evening,' he said.

Stratton said the assailant would almost certainly have been covered
with blood. Had anyone seen a man in blood-stained clothing late on
Saturday night?

He appealed to restaurants and café owners, asking if they
remembered serving Mr Elliott with food or drink that day, including
that late-night meat-pie supper.

Bradshaw watched from the wings as Stratton was questioned about
a possible motive and noted his reply that they were keeping an open
mind. He said Mr Elliott certainly had several pound notes in his
possession when he left home on Saturday morning but of course he
might have spent those during the day. He said he was wearing quite a
valuable watch but it was not stolen by the attacker.

The officers had their suspicions about Elliott's sexual preferences but decided not to openly speculate. They didn't want to risk losing any public sympathy for the victim - even at the expense of depriving themselves of possible valuable information from the homosexual community.

The nearest hint of this darker world was in a statement from Supt Rudin of Chesterfield's Town Division police, saying that all information would be treated in the strictest confidence. 'Nobody need be reluctant to come forward. We are not interested in who was out with whom that night. If they have seen anything we would like to hear about it,' he said.

News of the killing spread like wildfire around Chesterfield and the whole of Peak District. The day before the news broke the front page headlines of the local Derbyshire Times consisted of a grocer admitting fraud, a three pound trout caught in the Holme Brook, and a police sergeant retiring to Warsaw. Now the town was at the centre of a grisly murder and featuring prominently in the national media. Those who knew Elliott told the media he was well-liked and respected. In Chesterfield his closest friends were the Butler family who kept the Royal Oak Inn on the outskirts of town in Chatsworth Road, Brampton. Landlady Kit Butler said he was a frequent visitor while out on a run on his motor-bike and more recently his car. 'He was a quiet, generous man,' she told the Press. 'All he would have was a glass of shandy and he would never stay late into the evening.'

In the hamlet of Longstone, where he'd spent so many years, there was silent shock at the news. 'He hadn't an enemy in the world,' said Bernard Saunders, landlord of the White Lion. He said he used to help out behind the bar before moving to Bakewell. A regular was quoted as saying, 'If he had one fault it was that he was over-generous.'

The White Lion, Great Longstone. Elliott was a regular there

14

Monday

Police were out in force. All late homegoers were stopped and interviewed and all cars on roads between Chesterfield and Bakewell checked.

The appeal for information began to pay off. A barmaid at the Spread Eagle recognised Elliott from the newspapers and said he was a regular there. She said he was one of a group of men who liked to keep themselves to themselves.

A bus driver named Joe Hicks came forward to tell police about two men he saw climbing into a light-coloured bubble car at the terminus around 10pm. They were in suits. One was middle aged with glasses, whom he saw come out of the public toilets, the other much younger. The older man had opened the front of the vehicle to allow his companion to climb in. Hicks thought there was something incongruous about them. Maybe it was the age difference - forty years at least, he guessed. It just didn't seem right. And that image had stayed with him. Shown a picture of Elliott, Hicks replied, 'Yes, that's definitely him.'

Brian Cooper was another who contacted police. He'd driven along Clod Hall Lane on the night of the murder. He lived in Dore, a well-to-do village on the west side of Sheffield. Brian and his wife had been visiting her mother in Chesterfield. It was around midnight, and rather than travel back on the main roads, they had chosen the more direct cross-country route, listening to the radio and chatting about her mother's health. The lane was a blanket of darkness, needing headlights on full beam to see the way. Without warning, after going over the brow of a hill, their lights caught a bubble car parked on the opposite verge with its lights out. It was facing in the same direction as them, towards Curbar. Cooper braked quickly and as their Ford Zephyr passed, they saw a person standing at the front of the vehicle. He shielded away from the glare. It was a light-coloured three-wheeler, and in those brief few seconds they saw that the man was middle-aged, about 5ft 10, and wearing a suit. He appeared to be fiddling with the lock at the front.

'I wonder what's going off there?' Mrs Cooper had said.

'A bit of hanky panky I reckon,' he'd replied.

'Well there's not much room in there for that!' He'd peered into his mirror. 'He can't be in any trouble or else he would have flagged us down.' Police took them back to the road and the spot they pointed to was indeed where Elliott had been found.

Later, Bradshaw was in his office going through background checks on known violent offenders when the phone rang. It was the front desk. 'Hello Guv. There's a gentleman, if you want to call him that, just walked in off the street. Says he might have information pertinent to the Elliott murder.'

'Did you ask what it was?'

'Says he'll only speak to a senior officer. It's all a bit queer, if you get my drift.'

'Put him in the interview room. I'll be down in two.'

'Already have, Guv. Oh, and if you need a hand just gissa shout.' The sergeant chuckled and put the receiver down.

Bradshaw entered to find a middle-aged man staring at the floor with his head in his hands. He glanced up. He sure looked a sorry state. His face was misshapen with faded yellow bruising around the cheekbone. 'Sorry to have kept you. I'm Detective Inspector Bradshaw. Christ, what's happened to you?'

'Fractured jaw. I've had a good kicking.'

'What can I do for you?'

But the man was in no rush. 'Before we start, I need certain assurances.'

'Like what?'

'Like I won't be prosecuted for what I'm about to tell you. I've thought long and hard over this. I don't want to incriminate myself.'

'As I'm sure you can appreciate, I can't buy a pig in a poke. How can I give assurances 'til I know what it is you're admitting to?'

There was a delay while the man thought about his next move. Bradshaw thought he needed further prodding. 'I understand it's about the bubble car murder, that right? I think you've a duty to tell us if you've valuable information.'

'Look, I'm only bloody doing this 'cause some lunatic is running around killing people. I, er… think I might have run into the killer a week before the murder,' he said.

Bradshaw had already made a judgement about this fellow. He even bloody looked like Elliott for a start. He leaned forward for more. 'As you may probably be aware, my superiors have already said that any information of a sensitive nature will be treated in the strictest confidence. Tell me your name, sir, and we can go on from there.'

'William. William Atkinson.'

Even the same bloody Christian name!

'Can I call you Bill?'

The man nodded.

'So, last Saturday, then…'

'I'd been out for a few drinks and was walking back home near Queen's Park annexe. I heard a voice call out 'hello, Bill,' and thought I must know the guy. I was confronted by this man, or men, I'm not sure if he was alone…'

'And?'

'Well, I'll admit it. We chatted and I performed a sex act on him. Then before I could get up, he kicked five bells of shit out of me. I thought I was going to die but he suddenly ran off. Some passers-by looked after me and took me to the Boythorpe pub.'

'Would you be able to describe him?'

'Six feet tall, about 25 years old, and wearing a dark suit. His dark hair was brushed back. His voice seemed vaguely familiar, although I can't recall where I'd heard it before. It was dark. I only wish I could have seen his face. He said something about having to go back into the forces the next day - although he was not in uniform.'

'Where had you been drinking that evening?'

'The Spread Eagle.'

'Did you know Bill Elliott?'

'Can't say that I did, no…'

This was obviously of interest to detectives. And there seemed some remarkable coincidences. It happened close to where the bubble car was dumped, both victims were called Bill, both wore glasses, were of similar age and appearance, and on the nights they were attacked, both had been in the same pub. And they were both homosexual.

Bill Atkinson showing signs of the assault

However, identification of the attacker wasn't just thin. It was non-existent. They asked Atkinson if he minded accompanying them to the Spread Eagle on the remote chance his attacker might be drinking there. Regulars were questioned over several nights. Bradshaw made a mental note for undercover plain-clothes patrols at the park annexe each weekend from now on. The lads will love that, he thought.

How The Sheffield Star reported the attack on Bill Atkinson.
Was Elliot's killer responsible?

Police were reasonably pleased with the response to their plea for help. However, one vital piece of information still eluded them. What the hell were Elliott's movements the day he was killed? Where had he eaten that meal? Had he dined with his killer?

-15-

Around teatime that same day, Michael Copeland went to the park with a mate, Alan Pickering. Two younger girls were sitting outside the pavilion enjoying an ice cream. 'Can I have a lick?' Copeland said to a young brunette enjoying a vanilla cornet. The girl, who was only sixteen, was flattered by the older man's attention. She saw he was carrying that day's Daily Mirror.

'Only if you let me have a look inside your paper,' she flirted back.

They got chatting. Her name was Carol and she introduced her mate as Sylvia. They worked together as shop assistants in town. Sylvia read the signals and suggested to Pickering they both take a stroll.

Meanwhile Carol and Copeland walked around the cricket ground perimeter and sat on a bench reserved for members of Derbyshire County Cricket Club. He showed her the headlines. 'You seen this murder? Terrible, eh!' he said, shaking his head in disgust. They chatted and laughed for the rest of the evening. He told her he was on leave from the Army and had to return to Germany the following weekend. 'I've a lot to pack in,' he said. He asked if he could take her out the following evening. And she gave him her phone number.

For their first proper date, they met in town. He wore a windcheater and light trousers, with his usual combed back hair style modelled on the teenage heartthrob Paul Anka. She arrived in a summer dress and make-up, hurriedly applied after leaving the house to escape the disapproval of her father.

He took her on the bus to a miners' welfare club. He was a former haulage hand at Markham Colliery, near Chesterfield, but his membership was still active. It was a traditional, mostly male setting – the first time that she'd been inside such a place. The club was brightly lit with thick patterned carpets and various testimonials and photographs on the walls. Velvet curtains were drawn across the small stage used for concert nights and Bingo. It was Tuesday, always a quiet night. A group of men played cribbage on one table and the couple found a corner to be alone and chat. He'd bought her a soft drink because she was under-age, and a beer for himself, plus a shot of Martini which, away from any prying eyes, he slipped into her lemonade. She giggled.

She was already beginning to like him - a lot. They chatted and drank for two hours. He told her how he'd left school at 15 to work down the pit and how hard it was at first not just physically, but putting up with the practical jokes the men always played on new young recruits. 'They sent me to find a left-handed spanner and I was passed from pillar to post 'til I twigged,' he said. He opened up about his childhood and how unhappy he'd been.

'What about friends?'

'What about 'em?'

'Isn't there anyone close?'

He said he'd never had many friends. Most of his old school mates had either married or gone their separate ways - manual workers, down the pit, into factories. She hung on his every word.

He told her about his love of poetry and art. He'd never had formal training except the odd comment by the art teacher at school. 'I'm best at charcoal. It's more moody. I'll show you my sketches one day.'

'I'd like that,' she said.

Someone put a coin in the jukebox - A Big Hunk Of Love by Elvis. He kissed her for the first time and he could tell she was keen on maybe going further. He broke off. 'Are you a virgin?'

'It's for you to find out,' she said.

He confessed how shocked and disgusted he was when as a teenager he stumbled on his parents making love in their bedroom one day. 'I won't go into details, but it was so mucky,' he said.

Later that evening they found a secluded wood and made love for the first time. She perceived tension in him all the way through. Afterwards she hugged him for several minutes, sensing even at her tender age that he needed mothering as well as loving.

The CID circled a map of Chesterfield and tasked officers with the job of visiting every eating establishment within a five-mile radius of the centre. It was an onerous duty. There were hundreds of places selling food - posh restaurants, steak houses, cafes and market stalls.

Sergeant Andrew Wright volunteered to scour the south side of town. Before gaining his stripes, he was a beat bobby around the St Augustines council estate and knew that manor well. If truth be told, he was also aware there were far fewer establishments to visit in what was a predominately residential area.

On Derby Road was a fish and chip shop run by a woman called Irene Mitchell. He'd called there a number of times in the past, both for professional reasons, and to grab something to eat while on duty. Irene seemed to know everything that was going on in those parts and was a useful source of information for a beat constable.

Seventy-two hours after the discovery of the body, he called in on the off-chance that Elliott might have purchased his pie there on the day he died.

'Hello Irene.'

'Goodness me, what brings you back down here? I've just put some cod in... it'll be a few minutes yet,' she replied.

'No, it's business I'm afraid.' He showed her a photo of Elliott and asked if she'd ever seen him.

'Is this that murdered bloke?... can't say that I have - except for what I read in the papers.'

'Cast your mind back to Saturday night,' said Wright. 'Did you see anyone with blood stains? A customer perhaps?'

She stopped stirring the batter and thought for a second or two. 'As a matter of fact, I did. But it was only Michael Copeland. He's always in one scrape or another.'

Shortly after midnight Irene had been clearing up. She'd turned off the fryers and hot plates, had locked the door and was tilling up. A hammering on the window had made her jump. It was difficult to see who it was at first but as she got closer to the glass she had seen it was Michael Copeland.

She knew the Copeland family well. She'd been a friend of Michael's late mother and his father was a regular for a fish supper every Friday. Michael himself was a frequent caller on the way home from the pub. Knowing him, she'd been happy to open the door and let him inside. 'I thought you'd gone off to fight a war, young man,' she'd said.

'I'm starving, Rene. You got owt left?'

'Everything's switched off.'

'Not even any scraps?'

'All in the bin, sorry,' she'd replied.

'Oh come, on, just for me.'

'Michael. It's nearly half past midnight and I want to go to bed.'

He'd walked away a few yards but turned back.

'Can I have a match, then?'

She'd found some matches in a drawer and had handed them to him - 'Here. On the house.' When he lit a cigarette, she'd noticed that his hands were covered in blood. And the glow of the match had revealed blood on his face and collar.

'What on earth's gone off?' she'd asked. He'd dropped his head almost in shame and looked down at his hands as if it was the first time he'd noticed they were bleeding. 'I got rolled by some teddy boys. Don't worry I gave as good as I got.'

'You get home and sort yourself out,' she'd said, ushering him out the door.

Wright sensed a lead. 'So where does this Michael live?'

'On the Crescent... the third or fourth door along on the right,' she said.

'And what was he wearing that night?'

She remembered it was a light grey/green suit and grey leather shoes. He thanked her for her time and said goodbye.

***

The next morning Wright and a colleague knocked on the door of the Copeland semi. A strapping figure opened the door in a tee shirt and jeans, his biceps bulging under the sleeves.

'Are you Michael Copeland?'

'I am,' he replied.

'We're from Chesterfield Police. Mind if we come in?'

'Sure,' said Copeland opening the door wider.

They went to the kitchen where he'd just finished a tea and toast breakfast.

'I'd like you to tell me where you were on Saturday night,' said the sergeant.

'What's this about?'

'Just answer the question.'

Copeland looked at the ceiling and thought for a moment or two. 'Saturday... ah, yes. I went out to the Nag's Head on Derby Road until closing time. To be honest I had quite a lot to drink and felt a bit rough and came home alone at about a quarter to eleven.'

'Who were you with?'

'My mate Pickering.'

'And where does he live?'

'Park Road.'

'You mean where that bubble car crashed?'

'I suppose so, yeah.'

'Then what?'

'Then I went to bed.'

'Was anyone else at home that evening?'

'Nah.'

'We have reason to believe you were out in Derby Road after midnight and visited a fish and chip shop.'

'Ah, yes. Silly me. I told you I was the worse for wear. Yes I did... I felt a bit fuzzy and went for a walk around to clear my head.'

'Can you explain why you had blood stains on your face and knuckles?'

' Yeah... I ran into two teddy boys who had a go at me. As I say, I'd had a few drinks and I hit one of them... in self-defence, I might add. They ran off. There was quite a bit of blood.'

'Where did this happen?'

'Just outside my house.'

'Were there any witnesses?'

'I doubt it. It was quite late.'

'And do you know these teddy boys?'

'Never seen 'em before.'

'Can you describe them?'

'One was young. The other was tall... like I say, I'd had a lot to drink...'

'Show me your hands.'

Copeland held them out for examination.

The knuckle of the centre finger of the right hand was scabbed.

'How did you do this?'

'Hitting one of them,' he said.

The constable then spoke. 'Mind if we see your clothes from that evening?' They followed him up to his room and admired the art on every wall.

'This your stuff?' Copeland nodded. 'You're very talented,' said the constable. Copeland went to his wardrobe and produced a two-piece grey-green Lovat suit. 'Was this the one you wore on Saturday night?' asked Wright.

'Yep, the very one,' said Copeland.

Wright discovered specks of blood on the inside lining. It was smeared and he figured someone had tried to clean it off. Copeland merely shrugged.

'What about your shirt? Where's that?'

Copeland went to the wardrobe and produced a clean white shirt, freshly washed and ironed. 'My father's housekeeper Mrs Heath does all our washing... but I can show you my shoes if you like,' he said. The officers looked at each other and nodded.

He produced a pair of grey leather slip-ons. 'I was wearing these.' Wright examined three pairs of different shoes. None had any signs of blood, grass or mud.

'We'd like to take a formal statement, if you don't mind,' said Wright.

'Sure. No worries.'

A summary of Copeland's statement was collated on a card index file in what had hastily become the murder HQ at Beetwell Street. He was a person of interest, but no more than that. The trawl of eating outlets had failed to turn up any sighting of Elliott, much to the disappointment of detectives. And, almost inexplicably given its unique appearance, apart from bus driver Hicks, not one person reported seeing the bubble car at any point on that Saturday.

Routine enquiries in pubs, hotels and boarding houses, from people receiving treatment at hospitals, medical practitioners, patients on leave from mental hospitals, pawnbrokers, jewellers, toilet attendants, missing persons, people in custody, and a check on the movements of people known to have committed violent crimes, had all drawn a blank.

Bradshaw was left scratching his head. Motive was difficult to establish. There were no meaningful fingerprints from the car; Elliott's wallet containing some pound notes, his driving licence and car insurance certificate were missing, but the fact that the murderer didn't take his watch meant that robbery was less likely. He could only speculate that it must have been some sort of hate crime, or two male lovers falling out. He favoured a sexual motive based on the tin of rouge and Vaseline found in the car. Lab tests had come back confirming semen stains on the fly area of Elliott's trousers. And there was some make-up around the collar of his shirt.

An extensive search of the land where the body was found had revealed nothing. It was as if in the hours before he died, Elliott had been invisible. The investigation had ground to a virtual halt. Bradshaw, and the rest of the CID hierarchy, were desperate for a lead…

Only hours after police visited his home, Copeland took Carol on a walk to Barlow, a pretty village three miles north of Chesterfield. Sitting at the bus-stop he said, 'I've something to tell you.'

'I'm all ears.'

'I had a visit from the Old Bill today. Can you believe it, they thought I did that murder!' She raised her eyebrows.

'You what?'

'Someone snitched that I was covered in blood that night. Luckily, I could explain.' He told her about the fight with the teddy boys.

Just past Newbould, they got off the bus at Four Lane Ends and walked down a lane to a place she knew as Engine Hollow.

Engine Hollow Wood, Barlow

They walked for several miles over fields and through woods where they made love. Almost immediately he stood up and began walking around in circles, deeply agitated. He took his belt off and twisted it in his hands. Wondering what the hell was happening, she ran away, saying she wanted to go home. He caught her up, and grabbed her by the arm. She could see menace in his eyes and for a few moments feared for her safety. But then an immediate calm descended. He reached for her and stroked her face lovingly. They strolled through the trees hand in hand and rested on a fallen tree trunk. He began wringing his hands then looked her in the eye. 'Have you ever done anything wrong in your life... something you're deeply ashamed of?'

'I suppose. Can't think what, though.'

'Well I have. I have done something. I have got to tell someone about it. I want to tell you. I want to trust you. If I tell you, though, you have to promise not to tell anyone else.'

'Course not,' she said, adding 'but if you feel you can't trust me, then don't tell me.'

'No... I've got to tell someone, get it off my conscience.' There was a pause. 'Can't you guess?' he asked.

'No, I can't. How would I know? If you want to tell me you can.'

'Well, you might not see me again. I might be hanging from the gallows.'

'Don't be daft,' she replied, becoming concerned. She grabbed him by the hand and encouraged him to walk with her. They reached a bridge over a brook. She skipped across, but he stayed behind. She turned around and he was in the middle of the bridge with his arms out by his side like a child pretending to be an airplane. Then he shouted... 'I did that murder. I killed that man.'

The footbridge where Copeland 'confessed'

She went back and led him across. She told him not to be silly and go with her to get the bus. On the ride back he asked her if she'd taken him seriously. She didn't answer. Then he added, 'You see how clever I am? I only made that up to see if you loved me. But you don't, do you?'

She smiled at him without responding. Then he suddenly proposed to her. 'Will you marry me?' She thought he was joking but from his face and mannerisms she realised he was serious.

'We've only known each other a few days. I'm only 16… but maybe in two or three years time,' she said.

He saw her safely to her door and kissed her goodnight, whispering in her ear. 'You won't tell a soul what I said, will you?' She went inside and burst into tears. And, sobbing in the hall, told her parents every word of the conversation. They rang 999.

The call triggered a frisson of excitement among the hierarchy of the Derbyshire force. A squaddie had confessed to his girlfriend that he'd killed Elliott. What's more, on the night in question he was seen with blood on his hands.

'Let's pay him another visit,' said Bradshaw, grabbing his coat. Surmising that Copeland must be in a contrite state of mind, they adopted a friendly approach. There was no bashing down doors with police dogs but it was a dawn call. Bradshaw and the two officers who'd interviewed him previously knocked on his door at 6.30am. They'd obviously woken him up and they politely asked him to accompany them to the station. They wanted to go through his previous statement, they said. They allowed him to dress quickly while they searched his house and gathered clothing for forensic examination.

At the nick, the interview was carried out in a brightly-lit room and they offered him tea or coffee and a cigarette, all of which he declined. But he was agitated, constantly fidgeting and wringing his hands. They formally cautioned him, saying that anything he said would be taken down and might be used in evidence against him. He declined any legal representation, saying he'd got nothing to hide. They probed gently, asking him about his upbringing, school, Borstal and the Army. The questioning was designed to make him relax rather than glean any immediate confession. Copeland said that he'd been foolish getting into trouble for petty theft - but he'd never been violent. Half an hour in, Bradshaw ramped up the pressure by asking him to tell them where he was on the day - and night - of the Elliott murder.

'I've been through all this before,' said Copeland.

'Well, we think there's more you want to tell us,' said Bradshaw, keeping Copeland's woodland confession up his sleeve for the time being. The soldier repeated almost word for word everything he'd said in his previous statement but they pressed him for more. He finally admitted he HAD been in the town centre on the day in question. He said he'd gone to the market to buy a book on how to speak German. After a beer and a sarnie in a pub called The Peacock, he'd returned home to watch TV and get ready for the evening. He'd arranged to go drinking with an old mate, Alan Pickering, and one of Alan's brothers-in-law. After tea, he'd had a shower and changed into his new suit, grey slip-on shoes and a black cravat. He said they went first to The Whitecotes Inn and then onto The Nag's Head for three hours, where they watched a skiffle group. After downing three pints of draught beer and three or four bottles of light ale, at around 10.20 he'd had enough and walked home. He'd later popped out for some fresh air and to buy some chips and got involved in a fight with two teddy boys. The fish shop was closed, so he'd gone home to bed.

'Tell me more about these teddy boys.'

'One of them said, "look at that drunken fucker." I told them I'd give them one in the fucking gob in a bit. I went back and punched him. He stumbled back and said he didn't want any trouble. The smaller one just watched. They turned away and I walked home.'

Realising that Copeland was in no mood to confess, Bradshaw asked him about the walk with his girlfriend. 'Did you tell her that you'd done the Elliott murder?' Copeland was immediately taken aback. The bitch, he thought. She's grassed. 'That was a joke, a bit of fun. She was playing hard to get… I wanted to test her feelings, see if she was a serious thinking person. All I know about this murder is what I've read in the papers. You've got the wrong man if you think it was me.'

***

The interview lasted for 16 hours with several breaks. The officers rotated in turns to try to break him, but he remained steadfast in his denial. Leaving Copeland to stew for three hours, Bradshaw's bosses called a hurried conference of senior officers and invited detectives from Sheffield, the nearest major city.

'Fresh minds in case we've missed something,' said Bradshaw. He briefed the meeting. 'The situation we are in is not a happy one. We can establish beyond doubt that during the early hours of June 12, the period vital to our investigation, Copeland had blood spots on his face and part of his clothing. But we are not in a position to prove that the blood is of the same blood group as the victim. We can prove he had injuries to his knuckles but we can't disprove his explanation of how the injuries were caused. We have the sighting by Mr and Mrs Cooper of the bubble car in Clod Hall Lane in circumstances bringing doubtful possibilities of identification and we have some kind of a confession to a girl.

'Even when added together, it's not enough to charge him.'

There was little they could do but let him go. After Copeland left the station, Bradshaw, tired and disappointed, kicked the furniture in frustration. The day had started so promisingly. Now all they had was coincidence and conjecture. They were virtually back to square one.

They didn't need the brains of Poirot to know they needed more. Much, much more. It needed drastic measures. They decided to go house-to-house on over 20,000 properties in Chesterfield, Bakewell and Baslow. Everyone over 17 was interviewed and asked to complete a questionnaire. But that massive time-consuming and expensive trawl would yield little, except for solving a few minor crimes.

One thing they did learn was that the area surrounding Clod Hall Lane was a paradise for 'Peeping Toms' who even allocated to each other various stretches of moorland, watching homosexual activity, couples making love, or prostitutes who'd taken clients out from Sheffield. They were even equipped with field glasses, periscopes and walkie-talkies, signalling whether a particular couple was of interest.

Clod Hall Lane, a haven for 'Peeping Toms'

High on the detectives' priority was to find those teddy boys - if indeed they even existed. Police flooded the estate where Copeland lived. Surely someone must know something? Every door was knocked on - over one thousand homes. As a result, his name inevitably was on everyone's lips as a suspect. Meanwhile they put a 24-hour tail on him in the hope that he might somehow yield vital new evidence.

On Friday June 17th 1960, in the picture-postcard hamlet of Great Longstone in Derbyshire, two sisters wept as they buried their brother in the 13th century St Giles' Church they'd all attended as kids.

St Giles Church where Elliott was buried

The next day, a fortnight after arriving home, Copeland took the bus to Chesterfield Railway station to return to his regiment in Germany. In contrast to the sunshine when he arrived, the day was chilly and the skies were grey. He'd come full of hope and excitement. He was leaving under a cloud, literally and metaphorically. Was he a cold-blooded killer or some misunderstood 'Billy Liar' character living in a fantasy world?

No one was there to see him off... except for two detectives in plain clothes lurking in the shadows of the platform.

-20-

The day after Copeland left town, an article was published in a Sunday newspaper which gave an insight into how the man in the street - and the middle classes - viewed homosexuality.

***

It's worth recalling the backdrop. Arrests and prosecutions for homosexuality activity between men had been increasing since the War. In the nearby town of Rotherham, 17 men were rounded up in one go and pleaded guilty to 41 charges of homosexual sex. The judge called it a 'perfectly terrible story.'

For the public and many in authority this explosion of illegality was a worrying sign. The Government had feared the possibility of homosexual members of the Civil Service being blackmailed into giving state secrets to the Soviets.

This paranoia of 'reds under the beds' was magnified with the discovery of the Cambridge Five - a ring of spies who passed information to the Soviet Union during World War II - and the realisation that two of the group were gay.

The British war hero Alan Turing, the mathematician and Enigma codebreaker, reported a break-in in his home. Police discovered he was a closet gay and he was subsequently convicted of gross indecency, forced to undergo hormone therapy, and lost his security clearance. He later committed suicide by eating an apple laced with cyanide.

Two months later the Conservative Government set up a committee under an academic named Sir John Wolfenden to consider homosexuality and prostitution. It first met in September 1954 and over three years had 62 meetings. Much to many people's surprise and consternation, the committee recommended that 'homosexual behaviour between consenting adults above the age of 21 and in private should no longer be considered a criminal offence.' The Report caused much controversy. Indeed, one committee member publicly disassociated himself from the recommendations, expressing concern they would have 'serious effects' on the whole moral fabric of social life. An influential judge, Lord Devlin, argued passionately that the law should intervene in acts concerning morality - even if these were conducted in private. (He would later change that view.) The Government of Harold Macmilllan feared a public backlash and refused to implement Wolfenden. However, three years on, discussion rumbled on.

***

In the run up to a debate in Parliament - on Sunday June 26th 1960 - the Sunday Pictorial published a special report on the issue:-

One man in every twenty-five in Britain today is homosexual. A shocking figure? It is the estimate of the Wolfenden Committee on Vice. These men live in towns and villages all over the country. The problem of homosexuality is not confined to the big cities. This week Parliament debates a proposal by the Wolfenden Committee to change the law as it affects homosexuals. Its proposals to drive prostitutes off the streets have already become law. MPs will now debate the Committee's other controversial recommendation – THAT HOMOSEXUAL BEHAVIOUR BETWEEN CONSENTING ADULTS IN PRIVATE SHOULD NOT BE A CRIME.

If this became law it would change the lives of millions of men who are attracted to other men. Many of the them have sexual relations with each other which are at present criminal offences. What are homosexuals like? Can they be cured? Would a change in the law free them to increase in number? Are they a basic danger to society?

The newspaper hired a Harley Street consulting room to discuss those questions and filled it with a panel of mostly male professionals, some of whom were gay. The panel included an MP, a Magistrate, a leading sociologist, a surgeon and a priest.

'Homosexuality would spread like a prairie fire. They look on normal people as being the abnormal. Behind these perverted men is an ever-growing army of people who think it's a smart thing to do,' the MP told the meeting.

The homosexual surgeon intervened. 'The homosexual and the normal person should be treated in exactly the same way. It must be accepted that a homosexual wants to go to bed with another man just as a normal man wishes to do this with a woman.'

The priest observed there'd been no increase in homosexuality in countries such as Sweden and Holland where the laws had been changed. 'The present British laws give a completely unwarranted sense of fear and insecurity to a large number of people. This leads to a life

68

of promiscuity because homosexuals are afraid to have permanent relationships for fear of being caught or sent to prison. It takes away any basic human rights.'

The Magistrate said it was a popular misconception that all homosexuals looked and behaved like what he called 'nancy boys' or 'pansies.' The majority looked and acted perfectly normal in public. The fear of any parent was that their son would be seduced by an older man.

The surgeon said, 'Anyone can spot the obvious homosexuals - or queers, as most people call them. But if all homosexuals were recognisable then the streets would be crowded with mincing queers. There are a million of us, remember.'

The sociologist figured the likelihood of a man getting dragged into homosexuality was very slight. Sometimes it was hereditary, but normally it was acquired... acquired because a boy was brought up 'girlishly' by his mother perhaps.

It is not known whether or not Copeland, harbouring his own hatred of homosexuality, ever read that article. But the following Wednesday MPs again kicked the issue into the long grass. And it would be years before society was ready to reform.

PART TWO
GUENTHER HELMBRECHT

-21-

Hubert Lambert was about to retire for the evening when the phone rang. He was a captain in the Army's Special Investigation Branch (SIB) based at Celle, north of Hanover. Everyday disciplinary matters were usually handled by the military police, but the SIB were regarded as the Big Boys, called in to deal with the more serious stuff. There was no messing with them.

It was set up during the Second World War when 20 Scotland Yard detectives were enlisted in the Corps of Military Police to deal with pilfering of military stores within the British Expeditionary Force in France. Its role grew to become the name given to the detective branches of all three British military police arms for the Army, Navy and Air Force.

The call triggered an alarm. Two serious incidents. These had to be dealt with. Immediately. He threw some things into a bag, grabbed the keys to an Army Volkswagen, and motored across the North German plains to Verden, fifty miles away, and home to 700 British Army personnel situated in Caithness Barracks. Verden had a military tradition dating back to the 19th century, originally as a cavalry barracks. Its sprawl of low-rise redbrick buildings housed German horse-drawn artillery and later Wehrmacht artillery, part of the mighty German 180th Infantry Division, eventually crushed by the Allies towards the end of the Second World War.

With peace across Europe, rumour had it that as postings went, Verden was a cushy number, situated on the River Aller, and surrounded by beautiful countryside and rivers. There was only a remote prospect of Russia invading from the east. The mood there was laid back, with an emphasis on sport and physical education. There were plenty of leisure and entertainment facilities on the doorstep - beer halls, restaurants, cafés, cinema in English, bowling alleys, even at least one local brothel. Despite having a foreign army in their backyard, the natives were generally friendly. Many of the lads had German girlfriends: some would even go on to marry and settle there.

But as he motored across country, Lambert reflected that tonight's news could change all that, and, perhaps more importantly, have political implications, locally, nationally and even at Government level.

He pulled up at the main barracks entrance just after midnight and after showing his credentials to the sentry parked near the guardroom. It was misty and cold outside and he wished he'd worn something warmer. The camp was in darkness but a shaft of white light illuminated the night sky above the neighbouring woodland.

He walked through the wood and followed the path for 150 yards towards the arc lights. A crowd of people had gathered near a summerhouse – policemen, forensics, police photographers, onlookers, medical teams, media, even the fire brigade. There was a hum of whispered chat. Lambert edged through the throng to find the man in charge, a grey-haired overweight gentleman who identified himself as Kriminal Haupt-Kommissar (chief inspector) Freese.

'Can you fill me in what's happened here?' asked Lambert.

Freese looked at him with polite circumspection. To underline their special status, SIB officers were allowed to wear plain clothes on duty rather than uniform. Who was this shivering Englishman on a freezing autumn night wearing a summer windcheater? Lambert flashed his photo ID and immediately Freese became more accommodating, ushering the captain inside the summerhouse, where a paraffin heater was burning. 'It's much quieter in here... and warmer too!' They sat on the long wooden bench and soon realised they had a reasonably good grasp of each other's language, a huge bonus in the circumstances. Freese began briefing Lambert on what they knew so far.

'Earlier this evening, a local boy called Guenther Helmbrecht, two days away from his 16th birthday, took his girlfriend to the local Regina Cinema. I believe they saw the Hitchcock psychological thriller Rebecca. Have you seen it? I understand it is very good.' Lambert shook his head.

'The film ended about five or ten minutes to nine. Afterwards, they went for a stroll through this wood. We call it, rather imaginatively, Town Forest.'

Lambert smiled. 'They stopped here in this shelter but saw that another couple were inside kissing and cuddling and whatever... a young carpenter by the name of Adolf Struver and his girlfriend Helga

Hein. They are over there, giving my officers statements.

'Guenther and his girlfriend hovered outside for a while until the couple left to get a bus, and they themselves came inside here and were intimate.

'As you can obviously see, the shelter is open on one side facing the path. They'd been in here for about ten minutes when the girl, Inge Hoppe, who was also 15, saw a man walk slowly past. He looked in at them and then stopped by a tree ten yards further on.' Freese pointed to the right.

'This man hung around for a while and Fräulein Hoppe began to get worried. She suggested to Guenther they should go, but the boy replied that they needn't be afraid. It was her imagination, he said. She insisted they leave the shelter and walk the other way, along that dimly-lit woodland path over there. Immediately, they saw the man was following them. She pulled her boyfriend to one side to allow the man to pass, but without any warning he attacked Guenther in a vicious and sustained assault. Terrified, she fled, hearing her boyfriend shout 'Du Lump' (you rascal) at his attacker.

'She reached the road up there, 200 metres away, and saw the couple from the shelter at a bus-stop, talking to a man and a woman. She was obviously very distraught and told them about the attack but it was all a bit muddled. They followed her back to the forest, but in her distress, she led them the wrong way. By the time they found Guenther he was unconscious on the pathway covered in blood and bleeding heavily.

'The two men tried to revive him, even using perfume as some kind of smelling salts, but he did not respond. In desperation, they carried him to the road. A barbershop was still open and Inge ran inside to call us. Two of my men and a medic arrived in no time, but the teenager was, I'm afraid, already dead with numerous stab wounds to his chest and throat.'

He paused briefly almost out of respect.

'This is obviously a German criminal matter, but given the proximity to the camp...'

Lambert interrupted, shaking his head in disgust. 'If we find that it's a British Army person responsible I can assure you he'll be brought to justice.'

Freese nodded. They agreed to conduct a joint investigation, and to share and compare notes along the way. German police would handle the routine enquiries outside the barracks, including all liaison with the victim's family, whilst Lambert and his team would focus on the camp. They shook hands and agreed to meet again at first light to review any overnight developments and agree a plan of action.

The hut near where Guenther was murdered

Lambert walked back along the path to the barracks. He would now turn his attention to that other event that evening, the second incident reported to him in that phone call earlier. At the guardhouse, the sentry waved him through.

'I think you'll find everyone's inside here,' he said helpfully. Sure enough, Lambert found a soldier on a stretcher on the floor. He was dressed only in his underpants and surrounded by medical orderlies. His trousers were ripped to shreds. He was as white as the sheet that was supposed to be covering him but had fallen to the floor. His hands were covered in dried blood and the wooden floorboards were stained red.

Lambert had a reputation as a tough, no-nonsense operator. His earlier respectful deference to his German counterpart had now melted into angry belligerence. And his voice was loud. 'I WANT TO KNOW EXACTLY WHAT'S GONE ON HERE,' he shouted to no-one in particular.

Medic James Gilligan was the first to respond.

'He came back from town bleeding and staggering from a thigh wound and collapsed in the guardroom, sir. I've had a look at it and it's a sharp wound, probably with a knife. He's lost a lot of blood. I've made arrangements for him to be taken to a military hospital and we're hoping for a vehicle any minute.'

'What time was this?'

'We can't be precise just yet, sir. We think around ten. The military police are still collating information.' Lambert made a mental note that ten was soon after the boy was killed. 'Well, we need them to bloody hurry up.' Lambert bent down to speak to the injured man and shouted.

'WHAT'S YOUR NAME, SON?' The soldier was dazed and had to think about his response.

'Er, Copeland... er, Sir.'

'And what do you do?' It took several seconds to reply.

'Driver... sir.'

'Are you gonna tell me what happened, then?'

Copeland didn't speak. He just stared into space.

Warrant officer Ronald James intervened. 'If I can help, sir, I was the first person to see him when he arrived back at camp. I asked him how he came to be injured and he replied that he'd been attacked by two German civilians near a cinema. Teddy boys, he said.'

Lambert tried to engage Copeland again.

'Can you describe these two fellas?'

Again, it seemed like the words were washing over him. He was groggy and drifting into a sleepy state, either real or put on. But after appearing not to absorb the question, he was suddenly lucid.

'... one was my height, around six foot... he had a dark overcoat. The other was smaller... but he wore a suit.'

'So, what happened?' Copeland said nothing. He was back in a world of his own.

'If I can help, sir,' said James, 'he said the taller man said something like "are you English, Johnny?" and when he answered yes, the smaller man attacked him with a knife. That's about all we could get from him.'

75

Lambert looked frustrated. 'Well, best get him to hospital. We'll interview him when he can make more sense.'

The entrance to Caithness Barracks

-22-

The next day

A German police officer searches for clues

Dawn at the barracks was about to reveal a cold and misty Monday morning. A heavy dew nestled on the playing fields and the half-hidden rugby posts painted an eerie scene. Lambert's alarm went off at 6am. He'd only managed a few hours. Adrenaline and crime solving were not conducive to a restful night. A long day was almost guaranteed and he decided on a hearty breakfast. Wrapped in a borrowed trench coat, he made his way across the courtyard to the officers' dining room, leaving a vapour trail of breath in his wake. Inside, he helped himself to a 'full English' from the buffet, and joined two fellow officers at a table. News of the local kid's murder and the bleeding squaddie had rolled around the camp, but he resisted efforts by his contemporaries to chat about it, switching the subject to Army politics instead.

He called in at the Commanding Officer's office, and requested they retrieve Copeland's Army record for him to go through later, and then a driver ferried him to the grey local police headquarters five minutes away.

Freese had been up most of the night and was already at his desk. 'Ah, good timing, Captain… Coffee?'

Freese had progressed with some haste. He'd called at the murdered boy's parents, and despite the darkness, a team of officers had been roused from their homes to begin searching the immediate vicinity for clues. Two pathologists had already conducted a post mortem overnight and Freese had their preliminary report in front of him. He joked about German efficiency before revealing the ugly details.

'The poor boy suffered 27 stab wounds...' he said, opening a folder containing a hurriedly hand-written report from a Dr Adolf Schmidt, chief surgeon at the Pathological Institute of Bremen. He shook his head in almost disbelief. '... in the back, neck, throat, chest, abdomen, upper and lower arms and left thigh.' Freese paused for them both to take in the enormity of the wounds. 'The killer must be one angry man. And for what? The boy only started work a few weeks ago. Probably his first romance. And then this...'

He carried on reading, paraphrasing as he spoke. Three of the stab wounds had penetrated the boy's heart, whilst the lungs had been pierced several times.

'Dr Schmidt considers that death was due to blood escaping into the chest cavity from the stab wounds to the heart and that death ensued within a minute or two of the wounds to the heart being inflicted.' He looked up from the file. 'That will at least give small comfort to his family... and the people who tried to revive him. They are feeling guilty that perhaps they could have done more, he said.

Lambert nodded grimly. 'Any idea of the type of weapon? '

'According to Dr Schmidt, it was a thin, double-edged knife. I believe in English you call it a stiletto type? And the blows were struck downwards from the top right to the bottom left, indicating that the assailant was right-handed.

'In an hour or so we will begin searching the forest for the murder weapon. I am also arranging with the local authority to open up all the sewage manholes in Linderhooper Strasse and Artillerie Strasse, the two roads around the camp perimeter.'

Lambert felt obliged to offer help. 'I can provide mine detectors to search the forest. I'll get my men to hook up with you later. And please pass on my appreciation to Dr Schmidt and his colleague,' he said. The inspector acknowledged the recognition. 'Oh,' said Lambert. 'I think you need to know that we had a soldier arrive back shortly after the killing, himself suffering stab wounds. The facts are flimsy at the moment and I'm trying to find out more. There's a possibility he was might have been involved, but he's in a military hospital being treated.'

Freese was cheered by a semblance of a breakthrough. 'If you can get us his clothes, then as soon as the mist clears I can fix for a tracker dog to follow any scent. We've had good results in the past. And there's something else... we have a good witness.'

Freese revealed that among the crowd of onlookers who'd gathered at the scene after the murder was a 24-year-old civil servant called Guenther Marchlewski, who'd got a good view of the probable killer. He'd been walking along Linderhooper Strasse, heading for the bus-stop to go home and had seen a man standing motionless in the shadow of a tree, looking towards the camp piggeries. As he approached, the man had moved so as to keep the tree between them - purposely, he thought, to avoid identification. However, the man was near a street lamp and he'd had a good look at him. He could be precise about the time - 9.47pm - because he was aiming for the 9.50pm bus. Marchlewski described the man as six feet tall, around 25 years of age, slim, with dark hair and wearing a dark coat with his collar turned up. It matched the description given by Inge Hoppe of her boyfriend's killer. Both Lambert and Freese were convinced it was indeed the same man.

'When your suspect is out of hospital we can arrange an identity parade don't you think?' They swapped phone numbers and agreed to be in constant contact.

Lambert returned to base and immediately raided Copeland's locker. He took possession of his clothes, including the winter overcoat he'd worn the previous night, personal papers, letters and magazines, and retrieved the blooded trousers from the medical room for the tracking operation.

He wanted to familiarise himself with the camp layout and walked the perimeter, a sandy and brown soil. They were bounded on the south by Linderhooper Strasse, the main road into town; on the north and east was a forest, and in the west another road, Artillerie Strasse, where Copeland said he'd been attacked. On Linderhooper Strasse were the two barrack entrances - the main gate leading to the guardroom where Copeland collapsed, the other, the Medical Inspection Room. If he really had been attacked by yobs on the far side of the barracks, why hadn't he gone in the first entrance, the medical room gate, rather than stagger bleeding another 200 yards or so?

Mid morning, a police tracking specialist pulled up with a dog called Berko. With a circus of German police and British Army personnel in his wake, the handler, a man called Walk, led the dog to a random spot in the forest, 30 yards from the shelter. Walk presented the dog with Copeland's bloodied trousers which he sniffed excitedly. Almost at once, Berko, head down, led them to the shelter, spun around, and tracked his way to the exact spot where the attack took place. He sniffed the blood-stained path for a while and abruptly appeared to give up his task for the day. Then, without warning, he pulled away with urgency, his handler struggling to keep up on the extended lead. Berko led them down the track to the barracks perimeter. But instead of heading for the main gate, he turned left. The followers looked at each other bemused. If he was tracking Copeland's movements he was going off in the wrong direction! Berko sniffed his way along the fence for roughly 100 yards and stopped at a small hole. He tried to get through but couldn't. Walk pulled the wire apart with ease. There was an almost comical scene whereby Walk first pushed the dog through, then squeezed through himself, then Lambert, Freese, and the rest of the circus each in turn. Now inside the camp, Berko sniffed his way past the piggeries towards the main gate… but then lost the scent. 'What do you make of that?' asked Lambert.

'Not sure,' said Freese.

Berko hadn't led them to Copeland's quarters as they'd hoped. But he had uncovered a secret entrance - one that later would prove significant in tracing the Chesterfield soldier's movements.

Lambert had been given a tiny office off the main administration area and an assistant from the military police, a keen young officer called Grayson who eagerly presented him with a buff folder. 'You wanted Copeland's file, sir.'

Grayson left to fetch refreshments while Lambert began reading. Private Michael Copeland, from Chesterfield, Derbyshire, had joined the Army of his own volition, signing his recruitment papers in Ripon, North Yorkshire a year previously. He was given the number 23607595. After completing his military training, he was assigned to the No 1 Signal Regiment of the Royal Signals as a driver, serving at the Caithness Barracks.

Grayson arrived with a pot of tea and biscuits.

Lambert went back to the file. There were reams of statements and paperwork to suggest that the relationship with the locals wasn't as rosy as everyone had painted. Soon after Copeland had returned from home leave in the summer, two Army privates had been involved in a fight with German youths in the town centre and were stabbed, sustaining nasty but not life-threatening injuries. The military police report into the incident revealed that after the attack, Copeland had urged his buddies to go with him and 'sort the Kraut bastards out.' The next evening a group of 20 or so Brits had marched on the town and smashed up a bar, throwing stools and overturning tables. One German man had been attacked and kicked about the head and put in hospital for three weeks. A British signalman alleged that Copeland was responsible for the assault. He was arrested and interviewed by the Royal Military Police but there was insufficient evidence against him because the German witnesses had been unwilling to come forward. Officers read the riot act to the whole Regiment and warned of a lockdown if anyone stepped out of line again.

And then, another entry that Lambert wasn't expecting. It was from the Derbyshire Police Force in England. Marked Private and Confidential, it set out that Copeland had been questioned extensively about the murder of a local homosexual man but released through insufficient evidence. He'd 'confessed' to a girlfriend about the stabbing, but later denied he'd been serious. And on the night of the murder he'd been seen with blood on his hands, face and clothing. The police had asked the Army to look out for any of the victim's outstanding possessions, including a wallet, driving licence, and certificate of insurance for his bubble car.

It was the next entry that made Lambert lean forward in his chair. Copeland's explanation for the bloodstains in England that night was that he'd been attacked BY TWO TEDDY BOYS! This was precisely his story regarding his stab wounds only yesterday! Lambert let out a yell of delight. Surely, too much of a coincidence! He was convinced this must be his man. And he would now make it his mission to prove it – not just the murder in Germany, but the one in England too. 'Get me the contact details for Derbyshire Police in Chesterfield, right away.'

'Yes sir,' said Grayson, picking up the phone.

-24-

It had been an awful summer for Harry Copeland, his lad branded a murderer by gossip and tittle-tattle, plain-clothed coppers parked outside the house pretending they weren't there, reporters at the door every five minutes, plus the whole bloody estate grilled about the exploits of him and his family. The local newspaper had printed that a 'local man' had been interviewed for many hours by detectives but everyone knew who he was. Fingers pointing, tongues wagging. Even though his boy had not been charged, mud stuck. No smoke without fire, they all muttered. He'd read somewhere that the sins of the fathers were visited upon the children. This was the other way round.

But by the autumn things had died down. With little fresh to report, media interest in the Elliott murder had waned, and there was a grain of sympathy among friends and close neighbours at Harry's plight. He began to hold his head up again, to look people in the eye, and truthfully say his son was innocent until proven guilty.

But as the nights drew in, the leaves fell, and fireworks filled the November sky, all that was about to change. He was pottering about the house when there was a knock on the door. It was a reporter from the Daily Express. He wanted an interview about his son being stabbed in an attack by local youths in Germany. Harry went pale. 'What do you mean?' he said.

'Don't you know? He's in hospital.'

The journalist explained that the story had been reported in the German newspapers and picked up by Reuters, the international news agency. Every national newspaper in England would be on the doorstep soon. 'Let me take you for a drink and I'll tell you everything I know,' said the reporter.

Nobody from the Army or local police had told Harry about the incident. His main concern now was to find out if his son was all right. He was assured by the reporter that the injury was not life threatening and as far as he knew, he would be released from hospital soon.

News of the incident put the local newspaper in a legal quandary. The laws of libel prevented them from calling Copeland a 'murder suspect.' They could safely report he'd been stabbed, but not directly link him with the killing of the lad near the barracks. Instead, the Derbyshire

Times ran a carefully worded story:

The 22-year-old Chesterfield soldier who one day last June spent 16 hours at Chesterfield Police Station being interviewed in connection with the 'bubble car' murder, is in hospital in Germany with a stab wound. He has told the Army authorities that he was stabbed by Germans near his military camp.

Inquiries instituted by the Derbyshire Times in Bonn yesterday revealed that Copeland is recovering satisfactorily from the wound which he received on November 9th, and that he is expected to be released from hospital within a few days.

Unconfirmed reports from Germany say that on the same day that Copeland was wounded a young German couple were also attacked in the same wood, the youth, aged 15, later dying from his injuries. From his camp at Verden, the Chesterfield man was admitted to the British Military Hospital at Hanover and later transferred to a similar hospital at Hostert, near the Dutch border. A British Rhine Army spokesman in Bonn declined to give further details and at the War Office in London the Derbyshire Times was told the matter was being treated as sub-judice.

At his home in Chesterfield Michael Copeland's father said he'd heard nothing from official sources and had not had a letter from him for 15 weeks. 'I am completely in the dark. I am anxious to be told. What father wouldn't be?'

Harry appealed for donations to visit his son. He told reporters 'The only way I will find out anything is to go out there - but I need help. I can only raise part of the money. I am not paid very much.'

He wasn't the only party taken aback by the developments in Germany. Derbyshire Police were initially kept in the dark too. But a few days after the incident they received a detailed 'confidential' report via the War Office in London written by a Captain Lambert of the Special Investigation Branch. The SIB had no qualms in naming Copeland as a suspect in the murder of Guenther Helmbrecht. They were waiting to formally interview him after his release from hospital which would be any day soon, the report said. Reading the details in his office, Chief Inspector Bradshaw shook his head in disbelief that Copeland had again used a 'teddy boy' alibi for his wounds. Much as Bradshaw would love to have been involved, it was, for the moment at least, an Army matter. And this chap Lambert seemed to have the bit between his teeth.

-25-

Michael Copeland took off his hospital gown and began putting on his Army uniform. A few minutes earlier the ward doctor had told him he was free to leave. On the other side of the bedside curtain two military policemen waited to escort him back to camp. He gingerly lifted the dressing over his stitches to inspect the wound that snaked down his right thigh. Healing nicely, he thought. But that nine-inch scar would be a reminder every single day of events that night in Verden.

Lambert had prepared for this episode for many hours, going through statements, assembling evidence, and deciding on tactics for the interrogation. He'd converted a disused office in the guard block into an interview room with two chairs facing each other, and a desk and chair with a notepad and typewriter for Grayson to take notes.

Enquiries by the German police had in fact garnered very little. They were unable to find any witnesses to the alleged 'teddy boy' attack, and an extensive search in the woods, drains and manholes had failed to find the knife used in Guenther's murder. Checks against the sales in hardware stores failed to come up with anyone who'd purchased a long, thin knife.

Lambert and his team had achieved a breakthrough of sorts via aggressive interviewing of Army personnel and gentle probing of German civilians working there. Under the promise of immunity from any charges, British servicemen confessed that it was common practice to sneak out of camp via the hole in the fence unearthed by the police dog. Lambert established that Copeland, without authority, had in fact left the barracks TWICE that evening, almost certainly going 'through the hole.' There'd been no passes for him to leave that evening, but a telephonist had seen him arrive back at the Main Gate dressed in civilian clothes just before 9pm. And, shortly after, a roommate testified that Copeland had come in and put on a black overcoat and pair of gloves before leaving again. An hour later he'd staggered back into camp bleeding.

Lambert was alerted as soon as the military vehicle ferrying Copeland from hospital pulled up. He'd start off easy, he thought, in the faint hope that Copeland might want to free his conscience and get everything off his chest. If not, he would gradually turn the screw, even threatening

85

him if necessary. He wanted that confession.

Copeland was escorted in, walking with a slight limp, more out of habit than as a result of his injury.

Lambert greeted him with a strained smile. 'So, how was hospital grub, then?' Copeland acknowledged the greeting with a smirk, but kept quiet.

'I'm Captain Lambert and this is Lieutenant Grayson. I'm Commanding Officer of 70 Section of the Special Investigation Branch of the Royal Military Police based in Celle. You obviously know why we're here, and indeed why you're here. I must tell you I have reason to believe you were responsible for the death of Guenther Helmbrecht in the wood by the camp on November 13th this year. You're not obliged to say anything, but anything you do say may be used in evidence against you. Understand?'

Copeland merely shrugged his shoulders.

'Another thing. After this session I have arranged for three separate identity parades from people who were at the scene and who saw you there. So you might as well save us all a lot of trouble and confess right now.'

But Copeland was in no mood to admit to anything. 'That's right. Blame every murder on me. I know you lot.'

Lambert - 'It must be burning away inside…why don't you get it off your chest? The last thing I want is to turn one of our boys over to the Germans. Between you and me they're a nasty lot of bastards. They learned a lot of cruel methods in the war. They'll probably shoot you at dawn. Let's keep this in house, shall we?'

Copeland said nothing.

'Right. Let's start with your story. How do you explain your stab wound?'

'I've been through this a million times already. I was rolled by two Germans walking back to town. You have the descriptions.'

'Show us how it happened.'

Copeland got up and demonstrated how he saw the blow coming and half turned away. In doing so he had raised his right leg, thus receiving the stab wound to his thigh.

'We've interviewed half the bloody town and searched the area of this alleged attack ... and there's not a shred of evidence to support your story, not even a speck of blood.'

'Well, I don't expect you to believe me. No one ever does.'

'You're right-handed, yeah?'

'Yep.'

'I've studied the angles. You know what I think? Your explanation is physically impossible. I think your injury was self-inflicted with your right hand... what would've been the 28th blow to that poor boy. You were in such a rage, you were out of control... and accidentally stabbed yourself.'

'That's rubbish.'

'Tell me why you left the barracks that night.'

'I had a date...'

'Who with?'

'My girlfriend.'

'You left without authorisation. No pass was issued to you that night... look, we know all about the hole in the fence. Our little German police dog sniffed it out... and your clothing led him straight to the scene of the attack. You were there, just admit it.'

Copeland shifted in his chair, but remained silent.

'Come on Private. I know you want to tell me... you're not in England now, you know. You won't get away with anything here.'

Copeland just stared ahead of him, a vacant, empty stare as if he actually wasn't listening.

'Okay, let's ask you something else. If you were attacked near Ma's Café, as you say, why didn't you enter camp via the medical gate? Instead, you limped past it, bleeding and about to collapse, and into the main entrance.'

'No comment.'

'You could hardly use the hole in the fence again. You figured you would leave bloodstains on the fence and you would have needed to explain how you got your wound sitting around the campsite playing cribbage!'

'No comment.'

'I have reason to believe you recently owned a flick knife. Is that correct?'

'Yes.'

'Where is it now?'

'I lost it.'

'When?'

'Three weeks ago.'

'Where did you lose it?'

'That's a stupid question. If I knew, I would have it now.'

'Can you describe it?'

'No. If you want it that badly you can do me a favour and find it yourself.'

'Lieutenant. Pass me that buff coloured file, will you?'

Grayson got up and did as ordered. Lambert passed the folder to Copeland.

'Open it.'

Copeland didn't know what to expect. He followed instructions... and there in front of him was a post mortem photo of the boy, still with blood stains on his face.

'Look at him... tell me, what do you see? Tell me why on earth he should be murdered? Out with his girlfriend at the pictures... Sunday night. Why, Private, why?'

Copeland looked away and but didn't reply.

'Okay, then, look at the next photo.' Copeland flicked through some papers and there was a photograph of William Elliott, the Chesterfield victim. Again, it was taken on the mortician's slab.

Copeland was clearly taken by surprise and turned his head away in disgust.

'This was down to you as well, wasn't it?'

'That's out of order... no comment.'

'How do you sleep at night, eh son?'

'Who do you think you are, some sort of Sherlock Holmes? Just because you've three pips on your shoulder... you think you're some tin god.'

Lambert sensed that Copeland had now closed shop - stonewalling and sarcastic. Every attempt to engage him for the next ten minutes was met with a cocky, arrogant 'no comment.'

There was little Lambert could do but take him to the identity parade. Straightaway.

-26-

On December 2nd, 1960 the first of three identification parades was staged by the British Army with support from the German police. They waited for the sun to go down to make it as realistic as possible and shortly after 5pm, 11 men were set out in a line a few yards from the hut near where the murder took place. They were selected from soldiers in the camp and local German volunteers. They were all of broadly similar appearance and build; all had dark hair and were wearing overcoats with the collar turned up. Copeland was escorted to the scene and ordered to wear the coat he had on that night.

'Right,' said Lambert. 'Where do you want to stand?' Copeland thought for a minute and opted for position 11 in the line – one from the end.

Inge Hoppe, the 15-year-old girl who was with Guenther, waited with her father in a car nearby. When everyone was ready, they asked her to exit and she walked to the scene. Freese ushered her into the shelter. He could see she was nervous. He bent down to her level and reached out and held her hands.

'Inge, my love. There's no need to be afraid. We are all here to protect you… the police, the British Army and your parents. I want you to stand just here. We are going to ask these men to walk up to the shelter, peer into it, and then continue to a point further along the pathway. If you see the man who followed you that night please tell us. Do you understand?'

She nodded but was too emotional to speak. One by one the men came into view, stopped for a moment or two, then continued on. She stared intently at each. Some looked her in the eye; others, noting her delicate state, looked away. Copeland arrived, confident and carefree. He paused, stared at the rafters above her head, and moved on. After the 12th man went through, Freese asked her if she'd recognised anyone. She shook her head, saying they all looked the same.

'Don't worry. We're going to give you another try, much closer.' This time the same men were asked to stand in a single line facing the shelter. Copeland again selected the 11th position. Inge bravely walked the line, looking intently at the faces. At the end, she turned to walk back again. But after passing Copeland for the second time she became hysterical, running sobbing into the arms of her parents. 'It was one

90

of those two... I don't know, I can't be sure,' she cried. Legally, it was another negative – and a double blow for the investigators. Lambert's heart sank. Freese thanked her and she was led back to the car.

For the third parade, the same 12 men were gathered at Linderhooper Strasse - the spot where the eye-witness Marchlewski saw a man acting suspiciously on the night. The men were told to walk with a limp to the tree and around the trunk. Marchlewski was asked to replicate his walk along the pathway on the night of the murder. Again, Copeland opted to be the 11th man. The young civil servant studied each man in turn and beamed at Freese. 'The most likely one is Number 11.'

Back in the camp, Lambert tried to hide his disappointment by coming out guns blazing. 'That's it, son, it's all over for you. That German bloke nailed you good and proper.'

Copeland looked the captain in the eye and with smug arrogance replied, 'The girl didn't pick me. Why should I worry? If you think I was involved then you'd better prove it.' Lambert knew it was effectively game over. There was a moment of silence as he twiddled his thumbs. 'Tell me. Why did you insist on the 11th position in all three parades?' Copeland opened up, talking about his liking for animals and his intense dislike for human beings.

'You are asking all the questions, but you don't know any of the answers, do you!? I've had it rough all my life. My mother kept me waiting outside public houses when I was a small boy. I began to lose faith in humanity. I had more faith in my dog.

'He had to be put to sleep on the 11th of the month. And you know what? My second dog died on that day too. My mother also died on the 11th. I become particularly depressed on that date.'

The interrogation over, Lambert arranged a top-level phone call with his bosses in the War Office. They went over the evidence.

- Copeland's return to Barracks with a stab wound leading to the suspicion that the wound was self-inflicted when he stabbed Helmbrecht to death. If this was so, there was an absence of conclusive evidence to support that contention.

- The wounds on Helmbrecht were inflicted by a right-handed man. Copeland was right-handed but so were millions of others!

- His allegation that he was attacked by 'teddy boys' - identical to the explanation given to Derbyshire Police in the Elliott case.

- His return to Barracks in the region of 9pm was consistent with his return home after visiting a pub on the night of the Elliott murder and in each case he went out again almost immediately.

- The track to the camp by the police dog Berko, although not conclusive, was in some way consistent with the chain of events.

- The identification by Marchlewski.

It was all flimsy and speculative. Not a shred of proof, just mere conjecture. They just didn't have enough to charge him. Any judge or jury would throw it out immediately.

The brass decided that Copeland was a bad egg. They wanted him out and threw the book at him for the minor offences relating to leaving the camp. A week later he appeared before the commanding officer on three charges - that on Nov 13th he'd failed to book both out and in at the regimental guardroom; that he was out of barracks in civilian clothes without a permanent pass; and, drawing on a previous incident, he'd negligently driven a vehicle. He pleaded guilty to all three and was sentenced to 28 days.

Upon release from detention, on January 5th 1961, the Army decided he had a psychopathic personality and he was discharged and returned back home to Chesterfield. The War Office sent an urgent note to Derbyshire Police to that effect. Copeland took a job at his old pit, Markham Colliery.

Meanwhile Lambert had packed his things and returned to his base. Copeland would soon become a bad memory, one that had got away. He took one last lingering look at the disgraced soldier's file. One date stood out from the page, the day that William Arthur Elliott was murdered. June, 1960. On the 11th day of the month.

PART THREE

GEORGE STOBBS

27

Mansfeldt Road, Chesterfield
March 29 1961

It had been a worrying night for Josephine Stobbs, waking several times to check if her husband was beside her. Now dawn had broken and he still wasn't home. She looked out of the window and checked the drive. His car wasn't there.

George Stobbs had gone out around 9pm the night before, saying he had to sort out an urgent problem at the Trebor sweet factory in the centre of Chesterfield where he was an industrial chemist. That in itself wasn't unusual. The factory was always busy and had been creaking of late under the pressure of, amongst other things, making more than a hundred tons a week of Regal Crown lemon sweets and packing them for export to America. The factory was only five minutes in the car. And after such call outs he always came home, slipping into bed quietly so as not to disturb her.

She got up and put the kettle on, wondering what to do. What on earth could have happened? She decided to ring the factory. The main switchboard was closed, but she had an out-of-hours number which was answered by security. 'Hello, can you put me through to the laboratory, please?'

'I'm afraid there's no-one there. All the lights are out. Who's calling?'

'It's George Stobbs' wife. Is he on the premises?'

'I don't think so, Mrs Stobbs. I've been here all night and haven't seen him at all.'

She put the phone down, her eyes fixed on the receiver for several seconds. At precisely 7.20 am she dialled 999 to report him missing. The call was put through to Chesterfield Police Station and answered by the duty desk sergeant.

He wasn't unduly worried. Husbands staying out all night was hardly unusual. He tried to ease her concerns. Perhaps he'd popped into the factory and had gone for a drink, and maybe had one too many to drive home. 'He probably crashed on a mate's settee. I bet he's on his way home now.'

No, that wasn't her husband. He would have rung, or taken a taxi rather than stay out. The sergeant took the salient details and asked her to contact the station as soon as he arrived back.

The road where Stobbs lived

28

One hour later
Park Road, Chesterfield

Heather Simmonds, aged 11, lived on Park Road, just up from the spot where William Elliott's bubble car had crashed the previous summer. That incident - and the following media frenzy and scary playground gossip about murder in the neighbourhood - made her suspicious of any unusual activity in her road.

Shortly after 8am, Heather left home to go to school. She noticed a strange looking car parked outside her front door. It was a 1930s vintage Morris Oxford Six saloon, black with a coach body, huge headlights, a distinctive silver temperature gauge on the front, and a spare wheel fixed on the runner on the passenger side. She was sure she'd seen something similar in old TV films but couldn't remember what. Curiosity made her peep through the front passenger window which was wound fully down. The keys were still in the ignition, the glove compartment was open and she could make out a tobacco tin. On the front seat were a packet of cigarettes, a starting handle and a red spoon. The car intrigued her and she made a note of the make, colour and number - JN 230 - then went to school. All morning she wondered about the car and came to the conclusion it must be stolen. On the way home for lunch, she called in at the police station to report it. The desk sergeant commended her diligence and smiled politely, saying she would make a great detective. Over tea that evening, she discussed the car with her father. Walter Simmonds worked early shifts as a printer and he'd noticed the car too when he'd gone to work that day at 5.40am, but unlike his daughter had thought nothing more of it. None of the family had heard anything in the night, not even a door slamming. They agreed it must have coasted down the hill and been abandoned.

The Morris Oxford outside Heather's house

'You did the right thing, contacting the police like that. I'm proud of you,' said dad to daughter.

The Simmonds family weren't the only people to have noticed the car. Even earlier two local men - Alan Grainger and Frederick Pashley - saw it around 2.15am. And about 3am, night worker Ernest Walker registered it too while driving home from Matlock. It stayed with him because it was a very old car and was parked on the wrong side of the road, facing the town centre.

-29-

8.15am that day
Clod Hall Lane

About the same time a worried Josephine Stobbs was contacting police, lorry driver Joe Asher was lost in driving rain and mist whilst delivering goods to the Peak District. What's more, a flock of sheep was being herded across Clod Hall Lane which gave him the chance to study a map. He'd heard about the discovery of a body on that stretch of moorland road nine months previously and always wondered exactly where on this road it was found.

Then, unbelievably, on the grass verge was what appeared to be a man asleep. Or even worse… He climbed from his cab to investigate. The man was lifeless, on his back next to a wall with his right leg crossed over the left and fully clothed except for his jacket. He'd suffered severe head injuries. His braces were undone at the front and back. His shirt and waistcoat were stained with blood and earth and were rucked up his back. Loose grass had been arranged on his face in a deliberate, almost artistic way. Asher wondered what to do. The shepherd was now over the hill and the road deserted. He had no idea where the nearest phone box was but sped off to Baslow police station and reported the discovery to a Sgt Venables who went to the road and immediately closed it at both ends.

The stretch where the body was found

Within half an hour, a grim-faced Bradshaw was at the scene with fellow CID officers. Twenty minutes later David Price - the same Home Office pathologist employed on the Elliott murder - arrived too. It was depressingly familiar. The body was beside the same stone wall and only fifty yards from the spot where Elliott had been found. And there were those same ritualistic patterns of grass scattered across the head and body. You didn't need to be a detective to realise the killer had struck again. A carbon copy murder.

Taking care not to disturb evidence, Bradshaw bent down to examine the body more closely. The man was middle-aged with thinning hair. He even looked like Elliott. The head injuries were severe and there were bruises and abrasions to the face and neck. He noticed a wristlet watch on the man's left wrist which was still ticking. He noted that could be a help in identifying him with his next of kin. He put rubber gloves on to carefully search the pockets in the hope of finding a clue as to who he was. But they were empty.

In the Elliott case, there was evidence of tyre marks indicating that a vehicle had been driven on to the verge where the body was found. There was no such evidence here, and no sign that a struggle had taken place. The absence of blood, except for a small amount under the man's head, pointed to the injuries having been inflicted elsewhere and the body transported to Clod Hall Lane and dumped. No instrument or other weapon capable of inflicting the injuries were apparent. Bradshaw radioed back his findings to HQ, going straight through to his boss, the Head of CID. 'He's struck again, Guv…' A serial killer was on the loose.

The body was loaded into a green van and taken to Newholme Cottage Hospital in Bakewell preceded by cars carrying Dr Price and his secretary, and senior police officers.

An obvious line of enquiry was to check missing persons, which threw up the phone call from Mrs Stobbs earlier that morning. Her description of her husband matched the body found in the lane. Officers called at her home to break the tragic news.

At 3.15pm - 17 hours after she last saw her husband alive - she had the appalling experience of formally identifying him at the morgue. Almost immediately she left the district to return to her family in London. The Chesterfield house was left empty with shutters across the windows and would never be lived in by her again.

30

The Morris is towed away

The discovery turned the spotlight on little Heather Simmonds' astute detective work. Police descended on the car like flies. Forensic tests would reveal heavy bloodstaining on the upholstery and brain tissue on the back seat. There were also bloodstains on the interior panel of the offside rear door and the front of both rear mudguards. A bloodstained grey tweed overcoat and soiled grey jacket were found, along with a pair of gents' leather and canvas gloves, a groundsheet, a handkerchief, and two walking sticks, one of which had bloodstains. Unaccounted for, but known to have been in Stobbs' possession, were his driving licence, a Ministry of Transport Test Certificate, several pay slips, personal correspondence and a leather notecase. The Morris was examined for fingerprints but none were found. Clothing, articles in the car, and control samples of hair and blood etc were taken to the Home Office Forensic Science Laboratory but nothing that could assist in the identification of the murderer was found. All the blood samples were group 'A' - Stobbs' blood type - and all the tested hairs were his own.

Price carried out the post mortem at the same location as Elliott's - Newholme Hospital in Bakewell. The subject was found to be that of a healthy, well-built man, 5ft 10 ins tall. There were 19 marks of recent violence about the head and body and Price expressed the opinion that death had been caused by shock and cerebral laceration following and due to a compound fracture of the skull, accelerated by very severe bruising of the neck. Fractures were depressed towards the brain which was bruised and pulped.

'These injuries were inflicted with very great force indeed by a blunt instrument having a pointed and semi-circular surface. This could have been a boot or a shoe. Another group of injuries consisted of multiple bruises of the face which could have been caused by small localised surfaces such as a fist.

'A third group consisted of many scratches with dust impregnation of the skin at the front of the chest and abdomen. These, together with the displacement of clothing, lead me to conclude that the deceased had been dragged by the feet face downwards. A number of these scratches had been made during life, some after death. The fourth group were minor marks of injury on the arms and hands such as would be suffered in a brawl.'

Death took place between 12 and 24 hours prior to the discovery of the body. There was evidence to suggest the deceased was an 'active receptor male homosexual.' The examination revealed that he'd taken part in homosexual sex, either shortly before or after death, evidenced by lubricant and semen, although it was impossible to say if this was rape or consensual. Seminal matter was found on his vest, underpants, front and upper back of trousers and cuffs of the overcoat, also on the swab from the penis. Blood tests for alcohol revealed he'd consumed about three pints of beer.

31

It was certain that whoever killed George Stobbs transported his body to Clod Hall Lane in the Morris Oxford. It was vital for police to trace his - and the car's - movements that day. Immediately, piece by piece, step by step, detectives began pulling together his details including the shattering news for his family that he'd led a secret 'double life.'

***

George Gerald Stobbs was 48. He was born just before the outbreak of World War One, the son of an officer who served with the Royal Garrison Artillery on the battlefield. He was the eldest of four children and had a privileged background, with royal blood in his veins. Through his mother, he was a direct descendant of Edward the First. He grew up living among doctors and lawyers in the south London suburb of Dulwich where he attended the famous public school Dulwich College and was a star pupil in science.

At the age of 26, he followed his father into the forces, signing up with the Intelligence Corps, where he was a sergeant. During the Second World War he served in France, Belgium, Holland and Germany but never discussed his experiences with his family.

George Stobbs in his Army days

He later met Josephine, the daughter of a brilliant doctor with a practice in Wimpole Street. They married at Marylebone in February 1944, settled in London and went on to have two sons, Jeremy and Nicholas.

After the war he eventually ended up as an industrial chemist earning £1,300 a year at the East London factory of Trebor Ltd. At that time, they were the largest exporters of sweets in Britain, sending to 70 countries. His role was to supervise the production of existing products and develop new ones. Chemists controlled production and prescribed colours and flavours for the hundreds of different lines, such as Refreshers, Extra Strong Mints, Fruit Salads and Black Jacks. Even though it employed hundreds of people and exported sweets around the world, the 'spice factory' was quite primitive in many ways, boiling sugar and sweets over coke fires. It was hot and smelly work. In summer wasps, attracted by the sweet perfume and sugar, were a constant irritation. There were frequent breakdowns of machinery and shortages of ingredients, and decisions had to be made fast to keep the operation rolling.

Early in 1960 the firm asked George if he would be interested in transferring to the Chesterfield factory as a stop gap transfer. It occupied a former brewery in the heart of the town next to the railway station. The company had set up the Chesterfield operation during the war to protect their sweet-making from Nazi bombs. The chairman of the town council's development committee had written to Trebor extolling the virtues of the five-acre site, which he said was ideal to service all major British cities and handily placed next to a railway goods yard. It was exactly 150 miles from London, 25 miles north of Derby and 12 miles south of Sheffield. He'd claimed 16 million people lived within a 70-mile radius of the railway station, a greater population than within the same radius of Charing Cross in London.

By all accounts they were a happy family. George used to take his sons fishing and on day trips. With the boys away at boarding school, George agreed to relocate, alone at first, and on May 16th 1960, he loaded his suitcases and chugged north up the newly-completed M1 motorway in his newly-acquired 1930s vintage car. For a month the company put him up in a guinea-a-day room at The Clifton, a temperance hotel within walking distance of the factory, until he could find suitable accommodation for his wife and family. Staff there described him as one of the nicest guests they'd had.

The proprietress, Mrs Parker described him as polite, well-spoken and charming, and particular about his appearance. She said he had little in common with other guests. He seemed to spend most of his time in his room but did go out for his 'constitutional' late-night walk.

Colleagues found him an intelligent, well-spoken, and mild-tempered man and a gentleman. Richard Chapman, a foreman sugar boiler at Trebor, said he rarely missed a day at work and he thought it odd that he hadn't been in that day.

But there was a side to him that none of them knew. Alone in a strange town, George sampled the local night life and became part of a cabal of homosexual men who frequented town centre pubs. He'd arrived in Chesterfield a month before the Elliott murder and would have been aware of police activities and the risks of his secret lifestyle. Two months after moving up, he found furnished accommodation for himself and his family at Mansfeldt Road, Newbould, a residential road on the town's outskirts, and only a five-minute drive from his workplace.

**

Stobbs bought the classic car in a private sale in Torquay for £20. The Morris was much favoured by the middle-classes and retired Army officers for picnics and drives out to the countryside and he was delighted with the purchase at what he considered a bargain price. However, in the run-up to his murder, the car had been the source of trouble. A fortnight previously it had broken down and had to be towed to a garage for repair. Then, it was stolen from outside the Station Hotel near his workplace and later found on waste ground nearby.

On day of his death it had been in for a service at C.R. Bradley's Garage in Newbould, not far from his home. He took the bus after work and picked it up at around 6.30pm. Mr Bradley had previously suggested George buy a new model for around £250 but he'd replied that with two kids at an expensive boarding school he couldn't afford it.

From the garage, he drove home, but went out again at 8.50pm, lying to his wife that he was needed at the factory to sort out a problem. Mrs Stobbs would tell the inquest that her husband had arrived later than usual because he'd collected his car.

'We had supper and watched TV, a Peter Ustinov programme. He left home after it ended saying he was coming straight back. That was the last time I saw him alive and I reported him missing the next morning. He had never been out all night before and I had never once been to sleep before he came in.'

In fact, he'd driven to one of his favourite haunts, The Three Horse Shoes in Packer's Row in the heart of Chesterfield, where he'd spent most nights in those lonely first weeks, routinely arriving about 8pm, having two half-pints of bitter and leaving after an hour. He would usually return later for 'one for the road.' A barmaid there, Edna Muggeridge, said, 'I would often see him in the town centre late at night. He would come along Knifesmithgate, cross the road and go up Elder Way.'

On the night he disappeared he stood alone at the end of the tap room bar with a pint of bitter and slipping Queenie, the pub's crossbred bitch, mints he'd acquired from work. Police thought it significant that William Elliott was also a regular there. After an hour, Stobbs left and was next seen nearby around about 11 o'clock - an hour before he died. Joyce Mitchell, a barmaid at the Three Horse Shoes, was convinced she'd spotted him while on her way to the bus stop after finishing work. He was standing alone in the darkened market place near Harley's butcher's stall between 11.05 and 11.10pm.

However, that seemingly contradicted statements from two women who were certain they'd seen his car around 11am in St Augustines Crescent, the road where Michael Copeland happened to live.

One of his neighbours, Violet Cutts, told police she saw two men starting a large black car outside her home. A man wearing glasses was at the wheel, while another man cranked the car. She was certain about the time because after watching a television play she went outside to put out milk bottles. The lamp in the middle of the street was out but she said she could see the outline of large car with a small station wagon parked behind it.

'I heard the car start up at about 10.45pm. It was particularly noisy and chugged off up to the top of the street and then broke down again. They started it up again and it went towards Bacon Lane.'

Another neighbour, Mrs Yates, coming back from the Post Office around 11 o'clock, saw what most likely was the same car parked on the Crescent. 'It was a very rough night and I had my head down against the wind. I was walking in the road and was almost upon it before I saw it. I said to myself "what a damned old car." '

-32-

Following the disturbing news that a carbon copy killer had struck again - and that the victim's car had been seen outside his house - there was only one place police were going to kick-start their investigation. Michael Copeland. But the local press got there first. James Dodd, a reporter on the Derbyshire Times, knocked on Copeland's door as soon as his office heard there'd been another murder on the patch. Copeland was eating lunch.

'Have the police been to see you?' asked Dodd.

'No, why would they?'

'Another body's been found on Clod Hall Lane. It's very similar to the Elliott murder.'

Copeland looked surprised and said, 'Oh God, that means no sleep for me tonight.'

It wasn't until the next day that police raided his home and searched his two lockers at Markham Main Colliery. When he arrived home at 2.45pm he found two officers waiting for him. They'd been let in by the housekeeper. They asked him to accompany them to the station and he agreed after being allowed to make a cup of tea. They took possession of virtually his whole wardrobe for forensic examination.

The interview at the murder HQ at Chesterfield police station was conducted by Insp Frank Hulme and Det Con Derek Stonely. Copeland was angry and aggressive and for an hour replied to all questions with one word - 'Bingo.'

Where were you last night? Bingo. Who were you with? Bingo. Do you know or ever met George Stobbs? Bingo. And so it went on, hour after hour. Copeland was eventually allowed to go at 8.30pm, having spent virtually five and a half hours stonewalling. Then, on the staircase on his way out, he suddenly opted to talk. 'The police always seem to be picking on me,' he said. 'If you must know, I was out in Chesterfield last night. I was alone and had a few beers in a couple of pubs.' Asked which ones he replied, 'The Royal Oak.' (The Oak happened to be opposite where Stobbs had been seen that night.)

'I don't know what time I came out. Then I had a look around the shops and was home well before midnight.' At the bottom of the stairs

107

he added, 'I was home at quarter to eleven and I never went out again. I had nothing to do with this or any other murder.'

No evidence could be found to establish that he knew or had even met Stobbs. The killer's clothes would have been heavily bloodstained. Yet forensic checks on Copeland's clothing yielded nothing of value to the enquiry. Not for the first time, with clouds of suspicion hanging over him, Michael Copeland was allowed to go - with the police unable to nail him for what was now three murders.

-33-

Joy Adlington peered out from the drawing room of her grand manor house on the posh aristocratic Stubbin Estate. She didn't like what she saw. Her home was set in 40 acres near Wingerworth, four miles from Chesterfield. It was a quintessential upper-class English setting - summer garden parties on the lawns, surrounded by woodland, wildlife, swans coasting across the ornamental ponds and miniature lakes, and rolling farmland as far as the eye could see. Stubbin Court, with its two-storeys, ten bedrooms, large entrance hall, double spiral staircase, oak-panelled drawing rooms and marble fireplace, dated back more than 200 years. It was purchased by her husband, John, a wealthy property developer and Master of the High Peak hounds, in 1953, and would later host international equestrian events featuring the Royal family - Princess Anne and her then husband Captain Mark Phillips.

The Stubbin Estate

The lake on the Stubbin Estate

But today, the outside was bleak. The sun was almost set. Dark clouds raced across the sky and squalls of rain hammered on the mansion's seven bay windows. She'd hoped to take her Golden Labrador Sandy, and sheepdog Pincher, for their usual walk around the grounds. Instead, she headed into the nearby Gladwin Wood to shelter from the wind and showers. Tracking through the trees, she noticed a small pocket diary in the mud next to a rhododendron bush. She picked it up thinking it might offer a clue to the identity of poachers who were forever plaguing their lives. On the opening page was the neatly handwritten name George Gerald Stobbs and his address, Mansfeldt Road, Chesterfield. There was also a logo of the Trebor sweet manufacturers. 'Got him,' she thought and carried on with her walk. Over dinner she mentioned the find to her husband who was reading the Sheffield Star evening newspaper. The name Stobbs rang loud alarm bells. 'That's the guy found murdered in the Peak District today,' he said, reaching for the telephone to call police.

First on the scene was Bradshaw who asked Mrs Adlington to show him where she found the diary. He noted that the leaf mould and earth on the footpath had been disturbed and on closer inspection could make out apparent bloodstains on the ground and rhododendron bush. Branches of the undergrowth were broken and further likely bloodstains were on leaves and bushes up to two feet high. Bradshaw thanked her for her diligence and cordoned off the scene. He arranged for a search party to start work straight away under floodlights.

It was clear that the lady of the manor had stumbled on the spot where Stobbs had been murdered. The search would reveal a gruesome trail along 100 yards of woodland path - fragments of human brain tissue, a pair of shattered spectacles and a gold-coloured pencil that had become detached from the diary. Police followed the line of disturbed soil to the boundary with Gladwin Lane, a cul-de-sac running alongside the wood. It was obvious that a heavy object such as a body had been dragged along. At intervals were small heaps of dead leaves and bloodstained areas indicating where the killer had rested on his macabre journey.

The killer hauled the body over the wall

At the wall next to the lane there were small splashes of blood on the top stones and a pool of blood at the bottom showing the point where the body had been lifted onto the road. They found a penknife, a bunch of keys, including one from the 'AA', a ball-point pen and some coins. All of these would later be identified as belonging to George Stobbs. Further down, where the stream crossed the lane, they also discovered a parking ticket issued to Stobbs by Chesterfield Corporation.

Police were convinced that the killer had bundled the body into the car in the lane before dumping it at Clod Hall Lane eight miles away. There were no clues as to the perpetrator's identity but they could draw conclusions. The killer must have been strong, well-built and possibly tall to drag a human body so far along a rough, gamekeeper's path. Detectives were convinced that this accounted for the severe abrading of the deceased's chest. Footprints were size ten and heavily indented into the soft ground. The body was loaded in and out of a high-built car and the severity of the injuries also suggested considerable strength. The killer, if not a local man, had a detailed knowledge of local geography. The isolated estate was a popular haunt for courting couples and homosexuals. And after the murder he drove the body over narrow moorland roads before dumping it on Clod Hall Lane. From there, he drove to Park Road where he abandoned the Morris - once again suggesting that he either lived within walking distance or had parked his own getaway car nearby.

There was no reason for the murderer to risk driving his victim away from the woods. He could have easily have concealed the body much deeper in the undergrowth. It was almost as if he was teasing the police. Was this apeing of the Bubble Car Murder and the fact that both victims were near duplicates in appearance, character and behaviour an indication of a psychopath at work?

And what about the cars? Some officers figured the killer must have a fairly wide knowledge of motor vehicles. Neither the bubble car nor the Morris were particularly easy to drive. The Morris, for instance, had a floor starter and the gearbox had no synchromesh, so double de-clutching on gear changes was essential. The chance discovery of the diary, with a list of acquaintances and addresses, was the first break police had achieved in both murders. And at last, they now had a murder scene... one that yielded many clues. They set up nightly monitoring of Clod Hall Lane and patrols of Park Road and Stubbin Court. They also posted a 24-hour watch on Copeland's home. But there was a feeling that the horse had already bolted.

PART FOUR

THE INVESTIGATION

Serial killings naturally attract intense media scrutiny and Chesterfield provided a feast not just locally but for national newspapers and television too. Derbyshire Police made a number of appeals for information but an arrest was a long way off. And there were rumblings that this largely rural force was out of its depth in such a high-profile and complex criminal investigation. There were calls to 'bring in the Yard' - a reference to Scotland Yard's long-standing expertise in solving serious crime. The Sheffield Star asked, *Must we wait for a third murder before they are called in?*

The Derbyshire Times devoted an editorial to the issue. Headlined **'Murder and the Yard,'** it said:-

The question reflects widespread public concern throughout Derbyshire at the 'Murder in Duplicate' killing of a local man – murder carried out step-by-step in the same fashion as the still-unsolved Bubble Car Killing of last June.

It is no reflection on the sterling efforts of the county constabulary that people are demanding the employment of experts in homicide on these baffling cases. For whichever way one looks at these two killings, they are the work of a man (or men) with considerable cunning, a macabre sense of sardonic humour, and let's face it, a most unhealthy disrespect for the police.

To transport a battered body eight or nine miles from the murder spot in order to dump it in almost the same place as the previous victim; to drive the second victim's car a further nine miles to abandon it where the bubble-car was left; to do all this in each case in a distinctive, easily-recognised vehicle – all these could be the trade-marks of a man who is something more than a cunning killer.

What is needed here is a highly-experienced Scotland Yard Murder Squad, men accustomed to the behaviour of killers, and with ready access to other experts in the field of exploring the criminal mind. They would be still backed by the extensive local knowledge of the County Force – an essential factor in the investigation of crimes which have such obvious local links.

The cost of calling in a Scotland Yard team would now fall upon the ratepayers. But our inquiries this week suggest people are prepared to

*foot the bill to satisfy themselves everything possible is being done to
clear up these brutal crimes. As a matter of vital public concern, the
Derbyshire Times this week raised the question of calling in The Yard in
a questionnaire to the Chief Constable of Derbyshire, Mr W.E. Pitts.*

The following was his reply:-

*The responsibility for calling in officers from Scotland Yard is mine
and I would have no hesitation whatever in calling them in if I thought
the crime was beyond our resources. I am quite satisfied that we have the
detective officers in this Force who are trained and expert in any branch
of crime detection and who are intimately conversant with the geography
of the district and its people.*

*There is no question of local pride in this decision. We have the men
and the material. There would be no cost to the ratepayers if Scotland
Yard was called in. We have all the resources of our neighbouring forces
at our disposal and we have taken advantage of these. It is of course
impossible to disclose every line of inquiry the police are making but the
public can be assured that all police energies are being directed towards
a solution of these murders.*

The police were under huge pressure to produce a result - from
the public, politicians and the media. The brass threw unprecedented
resources at the case. Extra officers were drafted in and overtime
reached a record high. It was the biggest investigation ever carried out
by the Derbyshire Force. Around 50 officers were attached to the Murder
Squad alone with back up from an army of uniformed police on a daily
basis. Even so, a senior officer whispered to a local journalist that their
main hope was that routine enquiries might throw up new vital clues.
But it was a long shot.

A high-level conference was called with the Director of Public
Prosecutions. The central question was, did they have enough to charge
Michael Copeland? After much deliberation the answer from the lawyers
was an emphatic 'No.' To the layman, and most of the Murder Squad,
Copeland's involvement was obvious. Yet in strict legal terms, it was all
coincidence and conjecture without a shred of firm evidence to link him
with any of three crimes he'd been questioned about.

The murder team decided their main hope was to target the

homosexual population whom they were convinced were withholding information to protect their own. Under the headline The Shadow World, The Derbyshire Times commented:-

Police have admitted that they cannot rule out the possibility of a third murder. But we feel it our duty to inform the public - though the Police will not confirm this - that the victims of these killings are not completely innocent, normal citizens who have fallen foul of a homicidal maniac. Our own inquiries, and those of the National press, make it abundantly clear that the investigations into these two killings have impinged on the fringe of undercover activities among men in Chesterfield and district.

There has been talk of "shadow lives," "secret clubs," "double existences" and so on. A senior police officer was asked by the Derbyshire Times this week whether since the Bubble Car Killing, investigations had been undertaken to clear up the suggested homosexual clique in Chesterfield. We were told that there was no such clique.

Yet both murders have factors which can be explained in no other way. Men, travelling alone, were lured to lonely spots and killed with great force. They went apparently willingly in their own vehicles. The violence involved, the transportation of the bodies, the driving of strange vehicles, all virtually rule out the involvement of women in these crimes. Hints, suggestions and direct information all point in the same direction. To ignore these features of the two murders can only cause unnecessary alarm in the minds of the public at large who, quite naturally, fear that the killer might strike again.

It seemed police were learning all the time about this 'shadow world.' Det Insp Bradshaw would later report, 'it was made clear to us during these investigations that the social standing of an individual does not form a barrier between homosexuals and that males who are complete strangers will go together without hesitation to some isolated spot to commit indecent acts together. From this it seems reasonable to assume that by whatever pretence Stobbs had been lured to Gladwin Wood, the probability was that he had gone there willingly with his assailant. It was also clear that the sequence of events showed the time of such visit was in the region of 11pm or after and this in itself appears as a somewhat bizarre undertaking for a man of such intelligence.'

Plain-clothed officers were ordered to loiter in town centre pubs. One was drafted in to infiltrate the so-called secret 'cabal' of gay men pretending he was that way inclined and hoping to pick up gossip that might produce new clues. An un-named senior officer told local reporter John Raine, 'His enquiries will be carried out at great personal risk. The decoy will be a stranger to the area and although it might take some time, we hope to get some information about the murdered men and the killer.'

More than 800 homosexual and bi-sexual men - including closet gays and rent boys - were interviewed and offered an amnesty from prosecution if they provided information. Not all were local. One extraordinary consequence of the publicity over the murders was that homosexual men began flocking to the town in the hope of meeting like-minded people. Chesterfield became the gay capital of the North. Folk were afraid to visit public toilets through fear of being accosted. One Sunday paper described Chesterfield as the town where *'not only the steeple is bent.'*

Chesterfield became the focus national publicity with many of Fleet Street's big names arriving to write stories about a twisted town. Some of the locals were only too willing to exploit the notoriety. John Raine, who at that time was a local journalist, says today, 'As a young and gullible reporter, I remember being literally taken for a ride by a couple of local men who frequented the town centre benches and were rarely sober. They persuaded me they had vital information about the murders and would lead me to meet people who would give me a real scoop. Six hours later, having driven them in my VW Beetle on a 50-mile wild goose chase involving much buying of drinks, I returned to town with nothing.'

The police were torn in their attitude to the homosexual community. On the one hand they needed its help: on the other, the public were demanding action to clean up the streets. Queer bashing increased. One man was chased on his motor scooter by two masked men in a car and beaten up on Copeland's estate. At the same time, officers were losing patience with what many of them openly referred to as 'perverts.' They employed strong-arm tactics, and made threats to 'out' them to family and friends if they did not come up with information. There were accusations of bullying. Within a short period at least three bachelors committed suicide. One was a barber - described by his family as a very timid man who kept canaries and a budgie - who had a shop near the market. John Mart, 66, was found gassed in his premises on Low Pavement only a few hours after being interviewed by two murder squad detectives at Chesterfield Police Station. Straight from the police station, Mr Mart went to his shop, which he'd run for nearly 50 years, pulled down the shutters, locked the inner door, and gassed himself.

His sister, Minnie Dickenson, said her brother lived alone. He had lost his wife seven years previously; in all that time he'd led an active and happy life and had never been depressed.

The local paper reported that he'd once been assaulted in the shop by a soldier; it was described as a minor affair which received little attention.

The Coroner reported, 'I can only come to the conclusion that there must have been some worry which caused his mind to become temporarily unbalanced. It is not part of the coroner's duty and in fact it is highly undesirable to pry into the private lives of individuals.'

***

There were fears the carbon copy killer might strike again. And Copeland was their Number One - indeed only - suspect. Police adopted a controversial tactic. They decided to tail him night and day, watching his every move, under constant observation and hoping he would crack and confess. They followed his bus to the pit; waited for him at the gates, and crawled in a squad car behind his bus on the way home. They waited outside his house all night. If he met friends in the park, or in the pub, they were there. They sat behind him in the cinema, on the next table in cafés, even following him up the highway to Leeds when he tried to get some respite from the intense police scrutiny. Copeland once gave them the slip during a chase and reinforcements had to be called in. Another time in a car chase through the Chatsworth Estate, one of the officers in a squad car hailed him through a loud speaker, 'Come on Mike, you can do better than this.'

This ultra-surveillance went on for weeks. At first Copeland regarded it as a game, going into pubs by the front door and immediately exiting at the back, with officers in pursuit. Once, detectives stood at the bar near where Copeland was drinking with friends and a girl. In a voice loud enough for him to hear, they said, 'We'll have him soon. This will soon be over. Mick the Miller, Mick the Killer. You know, a funny thing happened to me on the way to the gallows. The bloke that did it is breathing down our necks right now.'

Copeland complained to police that they'd made him Public Enemy Number One in his home town, having to endure taunts from the public as well as police. Even kids avoided him in the street. Was this a legitimate crime solving tactic or harassment? As the days went by, Copeland became more and more angry at the attention and goading. There were frequent clashes with officers, some ending in punches being thrown. Two months after the Stobbs murder, he assaulted two policemen after they said something to him near his house. He wasn't charged, suggesting perhaps the police may have provoked the clash. His friends - and indeed the police - noticed a change in his appearance. He became thinner and pallid. The muscle he was noted for was fast disappearing. And the cocky arrogance was gone. In one pub he cried his heart out in full view of everyone. Even the 'undercover' detectives had to look away. For his own sanity he had to get the police off his back.

***

One night at Chesterfield Police station the phone went. It was Copeland asking to speak to a senior officer. Chief Inspector Peat came on the line and hunter and hunted had a friendly chat. They agreed to meet in the Commercial Hotel for a drink. Peat was intrigued by the contact and wondered what was in store. He found Copeland in a subdued but friendly mood, basically asking how the investigation was going and requesting that police give him some space. Just before closing time they went together to Chesterfield Police Station. Peat thought there was an outside chance of a confession. He introduced Copeland to a colleague, Sgt Evans.

'So, tell me lads... am I still the Number One suspect?' Neither officer replied. 'What's up? Cat got your tongues?' Copeland then ambiguously said, 'It's the violence of the devil when he rises inside the killer and he cannot control it. I can't control it. When the devil tells me to use violence I've got to use it.'

At this point Copeland asked if he could speak to the Chief Inspector in private and Evans left the room. They continued chatting. And mind-blowingly, Copeland admitted he killed the two Chesterfield men. It seemed the end of the hunt for Chesterfield's serial killer might be in sight. But he hadn't been cautioned. And there was nobody else in room, nor a recording of the conversation. When Evans returned, Peat said to both men, 'I don't know what I shall do now you've told me you killed Elliott and Stobbs.'

Copeland immediately replied, 'Have I?' He then walked up to Evans, looked him in the eye and said close-up to his face, 'Did you hear me say that?' Evans, who of course was out of the room at the time, could not reply. Then Copeland said he would like to leave.

The next morning, another high-level conference was held with Crown lawyers who ruled that since Copeland had carefully avoided saying how, when or where he had perpetrated the crimes, any prosecution was unlikely to succeed. Supporting evidence was required. The plot might have thickened, but they were effectively back to square one.

How one German paper reported suspicions over Copeland.

-35-

About that time, in a bar in town, Copeland began chatting to a girl. Her name was Marie. She was married, but in the throes of a separation. They started dating and soon became quite fond of each other. The trouble was, of course, they had little privacy. Wherever he took her, there were always plain-clothed officers in the background, even at their regular secret trysts at Old Whittington churchyard, and when they went for a walk in the country.

Old Whittington Church where Copeland hoped to marry

A normal romance was impossible. Throughout that summer they saw a lot of each other, even discussing marriage if circumstances eventually allowed. But several times she broke the relationship off. Copeland blamed the police for putting them both under strain.

At 5.40pm on September 27, 1961 - five months after the Stobbs killing - Copeland again turned up at Chesterfield Police Station asking to see the Superintendent. He wasn't available, but Det Insp Bradshaw happened to be on duty. He invited Copeland into his office and spoke to him in the presence of Det Sgt Downing. Copeland appeared humble and respectful, contrary to the arrogant Jack The Lad that Bradshaw had encountered earlier in the inquiry. The two officers, both experienced, were suspicious of his attitude and asked him why he'd come there.

Copeland asked why the police were still paying attention to his movements when all he wanted was to settle down into a peaceful life with his girlfriend. 'I'm unable to explain the torment you're putting me

121

though. You're driving me to suicide. You're all bloody depraved. You're following me everywhere.'

'Because, Michael, we know you were involved and it's in everybody's interest for you to come clean,' said Bradshaw.

There was a pause, both sides waiting for the other to speak. Copeland broke the silence.

'I want to tell you... I've associated with homosexuals.'

'To what extent?... would you like to tell us who they were?' asked Downing.

Copeland stayed silent.

'Are you a homosexual?'

'No, I am not. I have associated with them and that's sufficient. I'm not saying any more.'

Copeland looked down at his feet and pondered for a while. 'I know I'm a psychopath and I have a personality which could allow me to commit murder.'

'Are you suggesting that you could murder someone and not realise you had done it until afterwards?' asked Bradshaw.

'I have murdered no-one. If I had, I should know about it.'

After another pause, Copeland said he had more to say and asked if they would meet him later that night. And for them to bring along Inspector Peat - the officer he'd previously talked to in the pub. They agreed, and two hours later all three officers met Copeland outside his home. They drove under his directions to a village called Hundall, north of Chesterfield on the road to Dronfield, where he said he wanted to pick up his girlfriend Marie. She too squeezed into the car and they drove to a country lane and parked up. It was dark and autumnal outside. Copeland and his girl got out and asked the officers to follow them to a nearby spot called Grasscroft Wood. Whatever suspicions or fears the officers had, at least they were comforted by safety in numbers! On the edge of the wood, Copeland stopped, leaned on a fence, and said, 'What do you want me to say?'

'Only what you want us to hear, Michael,' said Bradshaw.

'I know I am only suspected of the murder because of what I told Mr Peat.'

He turned to the Chief Inspector.

'I told you, Mr Peat, that I killed Elliott and Stobbs. I know I'm a psychopath and I have a personality which could make me commit murder, but I haven't murdered anyone. I suppose I'm to blame for the way I have lived my life, although I always seek to put the blame somewhere else.'

He stopped for a moment, looked at Marie and squeezed her hand. 'I am nearer to God now than I've ever been and this is through her. And it is through her that I now realise how wrong I've been. Nobody ever listened to me. They've always shut the door on me. I get the feeling that I could commit murder and there are times when I do not even know myself. I have thought about this, but I don't think I could commit murder. I also want to say that I have associated with homosexuals and you know what that means. That's all I've got to say on the matter.'

The officers looked at each other. All hopes of a confession had vanished. They'd wasted their time and they trudged off back to the car leaving Copeland and Marie in the wood. In the car going back, they wondered what they'd accomplished.

'What was that all about?' sighed Bradshaw.

'At least he's admitted he's associated with queers,' said Downing.

'And that he's a psychopath and has a personality which could lead him to commit murder,' said Peat.

'So effing what?' said Bradshaw, not for the first time frustrated that his man was still out of his grasp. The surveillance would continue. Like a cobra compressing its prey, they would continue to squeeze him until he finally cracked. But this animal was fighting back. That weekend Copeland penned an article in the News of The World.

I believe I must be one of the unluckiest men in Britain. It sounds melodramatic, but it's true. Murder seems to follow me around. I have been involved in a fantastic chain of coincidences, a web of circumstances if you like. As a result, I know what they are saying: that I battered two men to death near Chesterfield and stabbed a boy in Germany when I was in the Army.

It's all lies... I hope that telling this story at last will do some good. I hope everybody in Chesterfield reads it. Perhaps it will lift this terrible cloud of suspicion hanging over me. I am entitled to that much. In one way, I am lucky. I have found a girl. She is a wonderful person; she understands me better than anyone else. I have a steady job now and hope to get married before too long. Then we'll live through the rest of this thing together. All we want is to be left alone so that we can live a normal life. Surely that's not too much to ask?

But any scintilla of sympathy for Copeland's plight was broken when three months later he was imprisoned for breaking into a local shop. For the time being at least, police could breathe a sigh of relief. Not only was a dangerous man off the streets, but their expensive and time-consuming watch on his movements could, for the time being at least, cease. Their enquiries ticked over. But in their heart of hearts, officers knew that the man responsible for three murders was now inside.

As Copeland sewed mail bags in Leicester Prison, on the outside life continued. The Space Race moved apace, Telstar transmitted its first live trans-Atlantic television signal, The Beatles released their first single, Love Me Do, Marilyn Monroe was found dead, and the world was brought to the brink of war in the Cuban Missile Crisis. And the hunt for the Crooked Spire Killer carried on.

On release from prison Copeland tried to rehabilitate himself, first down South and then in Leeds. But those spells away didn't succeed and by the autumn he found himself back in his home town. His first call was to Marie, begging for forgiveness and hoping to become an item again. The on-off relationship was back on - for the time being at least.

Police didn't reintroduce the round-the-clock surveillance but still monitored his movements on an ad-hoc basis. However, he felt hounded by the public. Men walked out of pubs when he arrived. Kids crossed to the other side of the street on the estate where he lived. His mental health began to suffer, deepening further when questioned by Nottinghamshire detectives about the murder of George Wilson, the manager of the Fox and Grapes in Sneinton, who was stabbed at the side door of his pub. He'd previously managed the Walton Hotel in Chesterfield, and they thought there might be a link. However, there was no evidence Copeland was involved or even knew the landlord.

Early in 1963, a further blow - Marie informed him she was breaking off their relationship for good. On February 19th he phoned her, pleading with her to change her mind. But she was adamant. Copeland visited a Chesterfield florist and ordered some daffodils to send to her. After selecting the bunch, he slipped a note inside. It was, effectively, a suicide note. He then went to the church in Old Whittington where they'd hoped to wed. He took with him a quarter bottle of whiskey and sleeping tablets. He was found unconscious in the churchyard.

The graveyard where Copeland was found unconscious

Medics at Chesterfield's Royal Hospital pumped his stomach and saved his life. The day after he was released, the sexton at the same church discovered him bleeding to death from a self-inflicted wound. He found Copeland on the floor in the boiler room with a deep gash in his arm. Again, hospital staff saved him, this time with a blood transfusion. They estimated he was 12-24 hours from dying.

Doctors told him he was a danger to himself and needed to be admitted to a mental institution. He agreed, and became a voluntary in-patient at The Pastures Hospital in Mickleover. However, he didn't stay long, discharging himself to start a new life - in Essex. Within weeks he was back in there again, this time sectioned by a court after being found guilty of violence. However, he escaped. The Daily Herald report, dated 5th July 1963 read:-

Police were last night hunting a 24-year-old man on the run from a mental hospital. They said he had a history of violence. Fair-haired Michael Copeland, of St Augustines Crescent, Chesterfield, escaped from The Pastures Hospital at Mickleover, Derbyshire, where he had been sent by a Romford court.

Earlier this year he walked out of the same hospital. He had been admitted as a voluntary patient after twice being found dangerously ill near a church at Old Whittington, Chesterfield. This all happened after his romance to his 21-year-old fiancée broke up. They were to have married at the church. In 1961, Copeland wrote: 'Murder seems to follow me around,' in an article for a Sunday newspaper. He became a suspect for the crimes that became known as the Carbon Copy and Bubble Car murders. But he was never charged and completely vindicated himself."

Copeland was eventually rounded up

-37-

In August 1963, the nation was immersed in one of the crimes of the century - the hijacking by a gang of a money train in Buckinghamshire which became known as The Great Train Robbery. Bradshaw was discussing the robbery with colleagues when the phone rang. It was Copeland, released from custody and now a free man. It was his first contact for well over a year.

He urgently wanted another meeting and they agreed a rendezvous near his own house. He found Copeland in a dejected and pitiable state - completely down and out, unemployed and without money. Wondering no doubt about the role police played in his demise, Bradshaw felt overwhelmingly sad for him and from that point on, virtually adopted him as a son. It was the start of an extraordinary and unorthodox friendship between a man suspected of vicious serial killings and the officer assigned to bring him to justice.

Bradshaw was to admit later, 'I was described as a father figure, a title which I certainly could not deny. I must confess that I was rather sorry for him and it was with these feelings of sympathy upon me that I gave him a lift in my car into the centre of Chesterfield where he hoped to meet a friend with whom he hoped to get lodgings.

'As he was about to leave the car I gave him ten shillings and told him that if he required help he knew where I was. I also gave him my home phone number. From that moment, I found myself in a situation where I was prepared to help him settle down and the subsequent association between us was to have far reaching effects.' But at no time during this early friendship did they discuss the murders.

Amid all this, there was a further distraction for Bradshaw and the rest of the now slimmed-down Murder Squad. An anonymous letter was delivered to Chesterfield Police Station. The envelope was addressed in block capitals "POLICE HEADQUARTERS, CHESTERFIELD" with the word "PRIVATE" written on the back. The envelope was postmarked Bakewell 6.30pm. September 24, 1963 but the letter inside was dated June. It was dirty and had the appearance of having been carried for some time in someone's pocket. It also had two corners torn off, including the writer's signature. The letter was headed "Dear Ann" and including the misspellings it read (the blank spaces are the torn-off parts):

I am sorry for not turning up for our last date. I got a bit scared of what you got to know about me. I am very frattened now because I was hoping it was going to be forgotten. I don't want anyone else to get to know about it. It has been hard to keep it to myself so long an then all of a sudden things start to come to life again. I had to kill hi ... I would have been ... anyway. His car was the only thing I could use to get away although I have never driven a bubble car before. Luck got me as far as it did. You will understand why I have stopped seeing you, it was not fair to ... husband. Goodbye for ...

Bradshaw was convinced the letter referred to the murder of Elliott and it was clear that even though it might be a hoax they had to investigate if only for elimination purposes. Police established it was posted at Baslow - where Copeland was then living - in the Bakewell Post Office collection area between 9am and 5.20pm on September 24, 1963, but neither the writer nor sender (if they were in fact different persons) were ever traced. As far as was possible, every woman named Ann in the Baslow area and every woman named Ann who had come to police notice or who had been interviewed in connection with the murder enquiries was interviewed but this led nowhere and the force concluded that the incident was a hoax. Copeland denied sending it and the letter and copies of his handwriting were sent to the Forensic Science Laboratory. Police were advised that in all probability the letter was written by someone other than Copeland. If so, it was another coincidence so soon after he'd arrived back on the scene.

***

Shortly after Fireworks Night, Copeland was involved in an argument in a pub. This coincided with another rift in his friendship with Marie and he was given notice to quit his furnished room following a quarrel with his landlord and landlady. He was then so full of self-pity and so low in spirit that Bradshaw feared he might try to take his life again. It was in that frame of mind that Copeland decided to clear his conscience and finally confess. He rang Bradshaw at home from a call box late on a Sunday night when the officer was off duty. He appeared emotional and asked if the Chief Inspector would meet him in town. They arranged to meet at Chesterfield Police Station at 10.30pm. Copeland was late, but the pair eventually talked in Bradshaw's office. 'So, what was so urgent to ring me on a Sunday night?'

'You must know...' Copeland paused as if to chose his words carefully.

'I… erm… I killed them all. Elliott, Stobbs and the German boy.'

'Do you realise what you're saying?'

Copeland nodded.

'You realise that as well as your friend I am a policeman and obliged to caution you.'

'Of course. I also know you're a very human person.'

'Well then, go ahead. Tell me your story if you wish.'

Copeland thought for a moment and then asked, 'Need I go into details?'

'If you want me to know, you tell me.'

'I killed them because it was something I hated. Elliott wanted to suck me.'

'Where did it happen?'

'Clod Hall Lane. Near a white gate.'

'What, where the body was found?'

'No. At the other end. I hit him and knocked him unconscious.'

'What did you hit him with?'

'My fist.'

'What happened then?'

'I got a stone from the wall and finished him off. Then I drove around with him in the car. I needed time to think. I went to the far side of the lane then came back and dumped the body.'

'Did you see anyone?'

'A car passed me where I dumped the body.'

'What happened then?'

'I drove to Park Road.'

'Where did the fish and chip shop come into it?'

'I left the car at the bottom of my road and then went in the chippie. I drove it round again afterwards to give myself time to think and then dumped it in Park Road where you lot found it the next day.'

'Did you know Elliott?'

'No.'

'Where did you pick him up?'

'I didn't pick him up. I met him in the bar at the Three Horse Shoes.'

'What time was that?'

'I dunno. Just before closing time, maybe.'

'How did it come about that you went with him?'

'He asked me to go with him in his car to a pub in Baslow.'

'Where was his car?'

'Right near the bus station.'

'When did he make the indecent suggestion?'

'He stopped the car on Clod Hall Lane and wanted to suck me… and that's why I killed him. I hate things like that.'

'Did all the assault take place in the car?'

'Yes.'

'Is there anything else you can tell me about Elliott?'

'I killed him because I hated him for what he stood for. I had his wallet and money, but I want you to understand that I didn't kill him for money.'

'How about Stobbs. What happened there?'

'I met him in the same place.'

'What time?'

'Can't remember, to be honest.'

'So what happened, then?'

'He spoke to me. I knew he was one of them and I hated him. It was premeditated as far as I am concerned. I decided to kill him because he belonged to something I hated most.'

'Whose idea was it to go to Stubbin Court?'

'Mine.'

'What happened when you got there?'

'We left the car just over the stream and then had a walk round. Then I hit him.'

'What with?'

'A hammer.'

'What happened to the hammer?'

'I can't say.'

'Do you mean you don't know, or you won't tell me?'

'I mean I won't tell you. If I do, you'll be out searching in the morning looking for evidence for court and I don't want that.'

Bradshaw was beginning to think the confession wasn't as comprehensive as he'd hoped.

'Answer me this. Where did you get the hammer?'

'I'm not prepared to say.'

'What did you do with the body?'

'I dragged it down the path by the feet, lifted it over the wall and then dragged it into the car. I then drove to Clod Hall Lane, dumped it and drove to Park Road.'

'What clothes were you wearing?'

'That green suit you had here and examined. I only got a few blood marks on it and then washed them off.'

'Did you do anything else?'

'I had the money out of his wallet, but again, I didn't kill him for money. I killed him for the reason I've already told you.'

'What was in the wallet apart from money?'

'Personal papers... you know, letters and things, and a driving licence.'

'What did you do with the wallets?'

'Burnt them.'

'What about the German boy? What happened there?'

'They were making love like I have seen my mother do many times with men. I hated them for it. I stabbed him. I don't know how many times. I just kept stabbing. Whilst I was doing it I stabbed myself in the leg.'

'What did you do with the knife?'

'I'm not saying. I'm not mental. I knew what I was doing.'

'OK... Do you wish to write down what we've discussed today?'

Copeland laughed. 'I'm not writing anything.'

'How about if I write it down and you just sign it?'

Copeland shrugged. 'If I did that, it would only cause trouble for my family and Marie. I'm not worried for myself but they would never live it down.'

'I can't understand why you should tell me a story like this and then not wish to write it down.'

Copeland paused to gather his thoughts. 'I think you're a sincere person and I want you to share this with me.'

'Do you wish to tell anyone else?'

'No, I'm not silly. I shall deny saying anything.'

They broke off for a cup of tea. It was 2am. The interview resumed half an hour later.

Bradshaw asked him if there was anything unusual about the clothing when he left Elliott on Clod Hall Lane. 'Not that I remember.'

'What about the shoes?'

'Ah, right, yeah. They pulled off in the car when I dragged him out.'

'About Stobbs. Did you go right away to Stubbin Court?'

'He took me home first. He dropped me off and I met him later.'

'Where?'

'At the end of my road.'

They were both tired and Copeland asked if he could stay the night in the cells. They agreed to resume their chat the following morning. Bradshaw went home but before going to bed made notes of their discussion.

At 8.30am he fetched Copeland from the cell and resumed by asking him if he could recall their conversation from earlier that morning. Copeland replied that of course he could. Bradshaw then read out the version from his notes and Copeland agreed that was an accurate account.

'I'm puzzled by Elliott, Michael. Did he do anything to commence his act of indecency?'

'He was bending over... look, I don't want you to think I was mental when I killed them. I knew what I was doing all right. I've never had a home life like anyone else and I wonder sometimes whether to tell my father all about it and what his reaction would be ... whether he would listen or run away and want nothing more to do with me.

'I think Marie knew all the time what was troubling me and that prevented us from finding true happiness. Do you think I'm bad, Mr Bradshaw?'

Bradshaw looked at him pitifully. 'I think there's good in everyone somewhere, Michael. You just don't seem to have tried to develop the good that may be in you.'

Copeland thought for a moment... 'I've broken every one of the Ten Commandments. At times I've thought that I would do something good and when it has come to doing it I have done something bad.'

He stopped and got up. 'I want to go home now, Mr Bradshaw.'

***

During the next fortnight he made several visits to the nick to see Bradshaw, always refusing to speak in the hearing of other officers and adamant he would not write or sign anything to incriminate himself. He sought help on how to obtain employment and, with his romance with Marie back on, even asked for advice on how to woo her. The problem for Bradshaw was that he was becoming more and more compromised by his unusual friendship. The relationship was more akin to a priest and a confessor than a cop and a killer. He couldn't act on the confessions without corroboration. And he was acutely embarrassed by the situation he was now in. Bradshaw decided to bug his own office and fit a microphone to his telephone with a loudspeaker connection to the floor below. If Copeland turned up again, they were ready to take down every word he said. But there was another twist in events.

Two weeks later, in the run-up to Christmas, Copeland went to a pub to meet Marie. But she ignored him and appeared to be with another man. He felt humiliated and slapped her in full view of other drinkers. The following night, Copeland dropped a glass of beer, splashing a man standing nearby, who said, 'Steady on, son.' Copeland punched him to the ground.

Then two days later he saw Marie walking arm in arm with a new boyfriend. He followed them and brutally assaulted the man, knocking him through the plate glass window of Chesterfield's biggest department store Eyres. A passing policeman witnessed the attack and arrested Copeland.

When he was taken in, Bradshaw was there to greet him and gave instructions he be charged with unlawful wounding and malicious damage. Appearing at Chesterfield Magistrates' Court he was remanded in custody and placed in police cells awaiting transport to prison. At 11.35am Copeland requested to talk to Bradshaw yet again.

Bradshaw went to the cells in a fiery mood. 'What do you want to see me about?'

'Some advice... the other Sunday.'

'You mean when you confessed to the three murders?'

'Yes... I think that you and the psychiatrist at Mickleover are the only ones who could get it out of me.'

'Well, I'm not discussing it here. Come up to my office and talk.'

The trap was laid. On the way, Bradshaw alerted two detectives - Sgt Downing and Det Con Nuttall - to listen from the squad room and monitor every word. Downing took down the questions and Nuttall noted the answers.

38

'How many people have you told about what I said the other Sunday?'

Bradshaw gathered his thoughts before answering that he had mentioned it... but only to a few selected people.

'I'm wondering whether to tell you anything else,' Copeland added.

The men downstairs were on tenterhooks. Would Copeland confess again but this time in their hearing?

'That is a matter for you. If you have anything to say, I'm here to listen,' said Bradshaw, nonchalant and with a poker face.

But there was still teasing from the suspect. 'If I told you everything, people would point their fingers and say I Told You So... maybe even you as well.'

'You know I wouldn't say that,' said Bradshaw.

'If I could change places with you, you could make the decision what to do!'

Bradshaw picked his words carefully. 'What can I say? I've known you for three years and you're not the same man as you were. You must know that yourself. Whether you will or whether you won't is a matter for you. But I think the sooner the better for all concerned.'

Copeland asked what the outcome would be.

'I don't know. You can only throw yourself on everyone's mercy. Surely it would be better than what you're doing now. You know that yourself. Sure, it will be difficult but if you've anything to say, it must come from your heart and must be the truth.'

'Yeah, but I'm afraid.'

'Of what?'

'What I told you the other Sunday...'

'That was the truth?'

'Yes.'

Copeland put his head in his hands. It was now just after 1pm. Bradshaw suggested they break for a bite and resume later. The prison guards had arrived to take Copeland but Bradshaw wanted one more try before releasing his quarry. At 2.30, everyone was back in position. Downstairs, pencils were poised.

'I told you the truth about not robbing Elliott and Stobbs. I didn't kill them for money. The truth is that I went out with the intention to meet a homo to rob. I met Elliott in Markham Road toilets and my intention wasn't to kill him… it was what he tried to do.'

Copeland then repeated his earlier confession - that they parked up near a white gate, that he knocked Elliott out with his fist in the car then finished him off with a stone - but adding that he first tried to strangle him. After dumping the body a car came racing by.

Regarding Stobbs, he said he met him in the Three Horse Shoes. 'My intention was to rob him. He said he was coming to town the next night. His approach was the obvious one for a homo. He said he would meet me in the Queen's Head.'

'When was it you first met him?'

'Three days before. The next night he didn't come. I went to Sheffield for a drink and when I came back I popped into The Rutland. When I came out, there he was walking past between the little shoe shop and the pub and we more or less resumed the meeting. I had it in my mind that night. We went to his car and he says "where do we go?"'

Stobbs drove to Copeland's home and waited in the car while he went inside his house to collect a hammer. 'We went to the Blue Stoops on the Matlock-Chesterfield Road. He went in and bought two bottles. We went to Stubbin Court and walked round. I made some pretext about going to his car. He never made any suggestions. There was nothing indecent.'

'So when did it happen?'

'Coming down the path. I struck him with the hammer. Death was instantaneous.'

'What did you do with the hammer?'

'As far as I know it's still at home… a claw hammer, but there're no traces of blood on it.'

As the interview continued, the officers downstairs ordered colleagues to search Copeland's home and bring in all hammers for inspection.

Bradshaw asked about the German boy.

'If there's anything that sticks in my conscience it's the killing of that German boy. If ever I could be called a brutal and callous person it was then.'

'What caused it?'

'Well, that's it. No sense or reason in it. Just to shake that chip off my shoulder. I didn't care who it was.'

'Which way did you get back to the camp?'

'Over or under the fence, I suppose. The knife is somewhere in the camp grounds.'

'Can it be found?'

'I won't tell you.'

Copeland then spoke about Captain Lambert, of the Army Special Investigation Branch, whom he described as a 'nasty man' because he'd shown him photographs of a corpse and then thrown them in his face.

They broke off for snacks and by the time the interview resumed, at 9pm, police had discovered five hammers at Copeland's home - including two claw hammers.

Bradshaw showed him the hammers. He declined to say whether the one he'd spoken about was there. He then said he'd probably thrown the hammer away with the starting handle in case of fingerprints.

'When you had a walk round Stubbin Court, where did you go?'

'To the pond.'

'Which? The little one?'

'The little one.'

'Where did you drink the beer?'

'Near the gate at the end of the lane. The one past the ford.'

'Where did you throw the bottles?'

'We just slung them over the wall near the holly tree.'

'What kind of bottles were they?'

'Half pint.'

***

Shortly before midnight, Bradshaw and his team compared notes and produced a full account of everything both men had said. 'It's pretty damning,' said Downing. 'Bang to rights in fact.' It had been stressed to Bradshaw that for any confession to be of evidential value it must of necessity bear relation to the facts. They examined what they had.

Regarding Elliott, they knew he was homosexual and Copeland had said his victim had wanted to commit an indecent act with him. The bus driver had seen two men getting into Elliott's car at the bus station near toilets where Copeland said he'd picked up Elliott. Copeland also said Elliott's shoes came off when he dragged the body out of the car on Clod Hall Lane and it was indisputable that the shoes were inside the bubble car when it was discovered on Park Road. According to Copeland, he and Elliott went to a white gate in Clod Hall Lane. There were such gates there. And they had the evidence of a Sheffield couple who saw two men near a bubble car. Copeland's visit to the fish and chip shop was also consistent with the owner's recollection. And not least of all, they had Copeland's admission regarding the driving of the bubble car and crashing it in Park Road.

'Let's go through the Stobbs case,' said Bradshaw.

Nuttall said again, they had proof he was homosexual which tied in with Copeland's version of events. They had evidence from staff at the Three Horses that Stobbs was a customer there which added weight to Copeland's admission that he'd met Stobbs there three days prior to his murder.

'And the evidence of the neighbours who saw a car answering the description of Stobbs' classic Morris fits Copeland's assertion that he was driven home before they went together to Stubbin Court.'

Copeland's references to the little pond or ornamental pond was a clear description of such a place near where Stobbs was murdered. And the abrading on his body tied in with his account of how he dragged the body through Gladwin Wood into the lane.

'And we know his leather notecase was missing and that Copeland

138

admitted he took what he said was his wallet.'

'How about Germany. What do we have there?' said Downing.

'The reference to sex. It's consistent with Copeland's reference to sex in both the Chesterfield murders and suggests a sex-hate motive in all three cases,' said Bradshaw. And of course there was Copeland's admission that he'd accidentally stabbed himself during the murder.

***

By the time he appeared in court for the assault charges, Michael Copeland had dramatically changed his name to Michael Crowther, and had moved to an address in Sunny Springs, Chesterfield. Derbyshire Quarter Sessions heard that he'd attacked Marie shouting, 'You think I'm a killer, a killer, a killer.'

His counsel, Brian Woods, said it was true his client had been the centre of 'certain enquiries' a few years previously, but no prosecution had ever been commenced against him - although he had attracted much attention to himself. 'The discarded lover has, I suppose, all through history been prone to show anger. As to his record, it is extensive, but is not, by and large, a record of violence.'

Sentencing him to 18 months, the Bench chairman, Graham Swanwick, QC, said, 'It seems to me that the whole of your trouble arose over your girlfriend. But you simply cannot be allowed to go round picking quarrels and attacking other men with whom she chooses to go with - otherwise we reach the law of the jungle. You are a person who apparently cannot and will not control yourself when your passions are aroused.'

With their man locked away, Derbyshire Police and the Crown's law officers had breathing space to assemble their case against Michael Copeland Crowther. The prosecution still felt they needed more. Every scrap of evidence would help.

With that in mind, Bradshaw went back to his case notes. Copeland had said they'd earlier stopped at the Blue Stoops and bought two half-pint bottles of ale which they drank near a gate in Gladwin Road and had discarded the bottles over a wall near a holly tree. Could police now find those bottles? It was a long shot. Nearly three years had elapsed since Stobbs' murder. Any litter might have been picked up or buried in leaf mould.

Bradshaw sent two detectives - Nuttall and Det Con Hall - to search the area near the gate where Copeland had said they drank the beer. Within minutes they located a holly tree near the wall and, remarkably, found a half-pint beer bottle in the undergrowth, five yards from the tree.

The lane and the holly tree

However, for the bottle to have any evidential value they had to establish that it could have been purchased from the Blue Stoops. They ran into an immediate setback. The pub said they'd stopped selling that kind of bottle three years previously. It had the name 'Warwick Brewery' embossed on it, and the police contacted the brewery for help. The bottling manager there described it as a half pint white flint crown bottle that had since been taken out of circulation and replaced by an amber version. However, they agreed that the old white bottle was delivered regularly to the Blue Stoops up until the end of 1961 - several months after the Stobbs murder. Bradshaw's hunch had paid off.

With the new evidence, conference after conference took place between the police, the Director of Public Prosecutions and Counsel. All they had were confessions. They were bereft of any physical evidence linking Copeland to the murders. They worked out nine points of similarity between the murders of the two men.

- Their homosexuality.

- Their injuries.

- Both found in Clod Hall Lane.

- Neither man was killed there.

- Grass had been scattered on their heads.

- Seminal staining on their clothing.

- Both their vehicles found on Park Road.

- Copious amounts of blood in both cars.

- Both last seen alive in Chesterfield town centre.

And so, after months of discussion and deliberation, they finally decided to put the coincidences forward for a jury to decide. On December 11th, 1964, four and a half years after the first murder, Bradshaw and Det Chief Supt Bowers drove to Winson Green Prison in Birmingham, where Copeland was serving his sentence, and charged him with all three murders. The fact that it was the 11th day of the month - that number again - was sheer coincidence.

How the local newspaper reported the charges

PART FIVE

THE COURT HEARINGS

39

At the beginning of 1965, the country was engrossed in the health of its former 'war hero' Prime Minister Sir Winston Churchill, who'd suffered a series of strokes. He was reported to be on his death bed and in fact would die on January 24th.

In the market town of Chesterfield however, the main centre of interest was the forthcoming trial of its alleged serial killer - the biggest case in the history of the county police.

Prosecuting Copeland for an overseas killing raised an interesting legal point. The Offences Against the Person Act of 1861 laid down that a murder on overseas territory could be tried at home - provided the accused "is a subject of Her Majesty." The prosecution had to prove therefore that Copeland was British. This was achieved by tracing his Army application which he signed when enlisting, in which he stated he was born on April 14th 1938 at Chesterfield of British parents.

The wheels of justice had ground slowly and the long time-lapse caused the prosecution huge problems. Witnesses had moved on; some were less sure of their recollections; Army personnel were now serving in different parts of the world, whilst others had left the Forces to take up new careers in Civvy Street. Two police officers, including Inspector Peat, who'd gone out pubbing with Copeland early in the investigation, had died (Peat with evidence still in his notebook).

Colonel Butcher, of the Army Special Investigation Branch, was assigned the task of tracking down service personnel witnesses in the Helmbrecht case, whilst Derbyshire Police sent an officer to Germany to liaise with the police there and to arrange for civilian witnesses to travel to England for the hearings.

Britain at that time was subject to a cumbersome and soon to be reformed legal system which effectively meant two hearings for the same offences - leading to duplication, huge costs and delays. Before a full trial could take place, magistrates had to decide if there was actually a case to answer in respect of all three murders. These so-called Committal Proceedings were mini trials, and began on January 11th - the date yet another coincidence - at Chesterfield County Magistrates Court.

Brian Woods, Copeland's counsel, said all three murder charges would be 'stoutly resisted.' Further confusion was caused by the court agreeing to his submission that they all be heard separately, which extended the committal proceedings to three weeks. This was a blow to the prosecution which had built its case on a string of related coincidences across all three killings.

A media circus descended on the town. The court was packed with press and public. Court staff were overwhelmed. Among those in the public gallery was Copeland's father Harry who attended every day. In the Chesterfield murder charges alone, depositions containing 28,000 words of evidence, representing roughly half a modern novel, were typed by the Deputy Clerk to the Justices. The Women's Voluntary Service set up a table in the courthouse and served snacks and more 1,500 cups of tea and coffee.

The dozen or so German contingent - including Fräulein Inge Hoppe, now in her 20s, who was with Guenther Helmbrecht when he was murdered - travelled together by train and ferry to Harwich and then by bus to Chesterfield. Local teachers acted as interpreters and social activity for the overseas visitors was arranged by the local authority at the behest of the police. They stayed at the Clifton Hotel - the same hotel, coincidentally, that George Stobbs lived in when he first came to Chesterfield. And in another bizarre twist of fate, the Civic Theatre next door to the hotel was showing a stage production of Rebecca - the film Inge had seen with Guenther on that fateful night in Verden.

Fräulein Inge Hoppe, aged 20

Opening the prosecution case for the murder of Elliott, Doiran Williams told the Magistrates, 'however wide your experience on the Bench, and however long you are destined to serve, it is doubtful whether you will ever come across a case more onerous or more likely to be investigated in the closest public scrutiny than this one. It is a story that explores the dark areas of the mind.

'The accused is a young man of some 26 years of age, and as you can see, of outstanding physique. He is a man whose very appearance suggests physical strength, and it will be the submission of the prosecution that the evidence relating to the deaths of the two men, William Arthur Elliott and George Gerard Stobbs, reveals how that strength was employed.'

Comparing their murders, Williams said, 'It is the contention of the prosecution that the similarities are so marked as to raise a very strong presumption that the same person committed both crimes. The similarities leave behind coincidence and they march into the region of undoubted connection.'

'Nine points of similarity between killings'

There were nine indisputable points of similarity that made the two Chesterfield murders into "Carbon Copy" ones said the prosecution when committal proceedings against 26-year-old ex-soldier Michael Copeland opened at Chesterfield yesterday.

Copeland, whose address was not revealed in court, is accused of the murders of William Arthur Elliott at Baslow in June 1960 and George Stobbs at Wingerworth in March, 1961.

WILLIAM ELLIOTT
Died at Baslow

GEORGE STOBBS
Died at Wingerworth

IN CAMERA

INJURIES

How the Sheffield Morning Telegraph reported the committal opening

Copeland, wearing a black leather jacket, sat impassively in the dock every day occasionally making notes and staring at the witnesses as they gave evidence against him. At one point he interrupted his former girlfriend Carol - now married - who said in the witness box that on a walk in the woods he'd taken off his belt and twisted it in his hands.

'That's a stinking lie,' he shouted from the dock and was ordered by the court police sergeant to pipe down. Parts of the evidence - from Bradshaw and from military personnel - were given in camera. At 7.43pm on the tenth and longest day of the proceedings, the evidence of the last witness - Chief Inspector Bradshaw - was completed. This too was taken in camera and then the press and public were readmitted. After hearing the mountain of evidence involving nearly 50 witnesses, the magistrates ruled that there was indeed a case to answer in respect of each charge.

Copeland was asked by the bench if he wished to saying anything. He exercised his right to reserve his defence. However, having remained mostly silent for three weeks, he stood up and made a 35-word statement. 'If the police really thought they were able to prove this charge, then there was nothing to stop them from doing so four years ago, when I would have been more able to defend myself.'

-40-

There was hardly a person in and around Chesterfield who hadn't heard the name Michael Copeland and his connection with the investigation into the Carbon Copy Killings. To prevent possible prejudice, his trial was shifted 100 miles south to the city of Birmingham. The hearing was set for the magnificent terracotta Victoria Law Courts in the heart of the city. The case was about to make history. In the realms of English criminal law, no one could recall a man being tried for three murders, particularly a young man at the tender age of 27.

Before the all-male jury was sworn in, the defence tried to have the German charge heard separately. Legal observers felt the boy's murder, with its added coincidences to the killings here, was crucial to the Crown's case. However, Mr Justice Ashworth - unlike the Magistrates in Chesterfield - ruled that all three be heard together, concluding that he wasn't satisfied that justice would be harmed. Copeland formally pleaded Not Guilty to all three charges.

The prosecution's central case was that Copeland had a hate motive connected with sex - heterosexual and homosexual - citing his own admission regarding the German boy, 'they were making love and I hated them for it.' The Crown claimed he had a two-sided character, 'one side poetic and artistic; then on the other side, something terrible he could not control.'

Day after day, the jury heard from scores of witnesses from Chesterfield, the Forces, and Germany; his statements to police admitting his involvement; even evidence from a prison hospital official that Copeland had told him he had a wild temper at times; that he had a killer instinct; and if the truth were known he would be put away for a long time. 'The shock of it would kill my father,' he was alleged to have said.

In his final speech for the Crown, Graham Swanwick, QC, told the jury that Copeland's alleged confessions lay at the heart of the case. 'If these confessions are genuine, that is the end of each of these three cases because they are complete confessions to murder.'

The defence strategy was unusual but simple. It accepted from the outset that Copeland had indeed confessed to the crimes, and that

149

police accounts were accurate. But Copeland claimed this was all part of his masterplan to get them off his back. His theory was this: by admitting the crimes he knew they would charge him. But he'd planted holes and inconsistencies in the statements so that any jury would see through them and acquit. Then his name would be cleared forever.
It was an extraordinary and high-risk tactic. If found guilty, the only punishment available to the court would be the hangman's noose. He might have refused to sign his statements, but was he in effect signing his own death warrant?

For Copeland, Rudolph Lyons, QC, quoted from Shakespeare and used flowery language to try to convince the jury to find him not guilty. He said Copeland had likened himself to Macbeth or Richard III, but he might have been thinking of Hamlet in that autumn of 1963. 'For three years he'd suffered the slings and arrows of outrageous fortune and the result of his submission was that his health was ruined and his life had become an utter misery.'

He argued that apart from the confessions, the prosecution case was only supported by the coincidences that he'd received injuries on the nights two of the victims were murdered.

'The prosecution are saying such coincidences don't happen. Don't they? Don't strange coincidences happen to each and every one of us sometime in our lives?' He drew attention to how the number 11 had featured in the case.

'The prosecution have seized on the fact that Elliott was killed on June 11th to suggest here was a man who went almost mad on the 11th of the month. Copeland's mother had died on the 11th, he'd claimed his dog had died on that date, and he insisted on taking position 11 in the German identity parades.

'I do not suppose anybody is so uncharitable as to suggest that the police deliberately chose the 11th as the day on which to charge him. The odds of that happening were 30-1. And that is not all. When did the committal proceedings at Chesterfield begin? It was January 11th 1965. Any bookmaker at Aintree last Saturday would tell you the odds against that happening were 900-1. But it came up!

'Over 200 years ago, a poet called Pope wrote that all looks yellow to the jaundiced eye. Had he been alive at the present time and been able to attend this trial he would, you may think, have found a host of examples to illustrate the eternal truth of those words. Once suspicion has attached itself to a person, it's very easy, is it not, to go to the microscope every time there is a piece of evidence and read something sinister into it?'

He said key prosecution witnesses had been discredited, including Captain Lambert of the Army's Special Investigation Branch, and Carol - once Copeland's girlfriend - to whom he allegedly confessed in the woods, 'perhaps the most vindictive witness in this case.' She'd said Copeland was a murderer, and she was terrified of him, but she had nevertheless continued to see him and have intercourse with him almost every single day until he went back to Germany. She'd then engaged for months in affectionate correspondence in which the question of marriage was discussed.

He said the accused had been subjected to a type of refined torture that even ancient China never devised - trailing him, harrowing him, haunting him 24 hours a day, taunting him day after day, month after month, ruthlessly ruining his health, ruining his prospective marriage, rendering him unable to keep in work. He'd twice attempted to commit suicide and had twice been in a mental hospital. The prosecution, he claimed, had year after year sat on the charges, willing to wound, but afraid to strike.

'And yet it was only this year, when both mentally and in spirit he was a mere shell of what he was in 1961, ill-equipped to defend himself and deal with events of five years ago, that the prosecution was launched,' said Lyons.

Copeland spent 17 hours in the witness box and was often rambling and incoherent in his replies, far from the arrogant, cocky solider of five years previously. His counsel said he'd clearly not recovered his formal mental faculties and had been labouring under a handicap in meeting these 'stale charges.'

Lyons fixed his eyes on the jury and said, 'You watched him carefully during that long ordeal in the witness box, utterly spiritless, lethargic, almost as though he was under the influence of drugs, allowing questions to go over his head, as often as not clearly unable to assimilate the questions being asked.

'I am not seeking your sympathy. It is a question of fact. I submit it is quite unreal to criticise him now that he has been broken on the wheel of cross-examination. You are not dealing with an educated man in normal health. It would be quite unreal and dangerous to hold inconsistencies against him.'

Summing up, the judge reminded the jury there were 16 instances where Copeland said he made deliberate mistakes in his confessions. These included that Copeland stated he'd finished Elliott off with a stone, when the evidence showed otherwise; alleging he'd parked the bubble car home near his home, arguing this was not so because someone would definitely have spotted it; that he'd picked up Stobbs at the Three Horseshoes just before closing and staying half an hour drinking when that would have been impossible because of the drinking laws.

'The defence case was that this was a last desperate effort of a man who had been persecuted - persecuted two and a half years or more - who could not get rid of the awful shadow wrecking his life. The judge said the Crown's case on the confessions was that they were those of a guilty man who knew what he had done; who was the only person in the world who could know all that had been done; and that he was a guilty person who could not carry his burden any longer.

'Sometimes there arises in the human mind a desire for what is sometimes called expiation. You want to wipe the slate clean. The Crown go on to say there may be mistakes here, but they are mistakes which are due to forgetfulness and they say it is inconceivable that in the autumn of 1963 a man going downhill mentally, who has twice attempted suicide, could remember details from newspapers - not one paper, but several - details which enabled him to make a confession as to the circumstances of the crime, which, in some respects, fit like a glove.

'Whatever your view about the confessions, this much is clear - the uttering of those confessions, and the devising of them with their two-fold purpose, shows the author was someone who had intelligence.'

After a hearing lasting 14 days, the jury were finally sent out to consider their verdicts. The judge told them they were engaged on a task of grave responsibility. There was no doubt all three had been murdered. The question they must decide was whether or not it had been proven beyond reasonable doubt that Copeland was the killer.

**

It was 2.42pm by the courtroom clock - three hours and seven minutes after they'd retired - when the twelve men filed back to the hushed and expectant courtroom. Copeland, in a black unbuttoned shirt and wearing his favourite black leather jacket, stood to attention. Pale, but showing no sign of emotion, he stood rigid with his legs apart, his huge hands clasped behind his back, as the foreman announced the three verdicts.

To the murder of Guenther Helmbrecht - Guilty.

To the murder of William Arthur Elliott - Guilty.

To the murder of George Gerard Stobbs - Guilty.

His 63-year-old father Harry rose quickly from his seat in the public gallery from which he'd looked down day after day at his son flanked always by four prison officers in the dock. He left the courtroom before the judge could pass sentence.

Asked by Mr Justice Ashworth if he had anything to say, his son replied, 'No.' And in that sombre piece of judicial ritual, the usher stepped forward with a black cap laid out on a bed of silk and placed it on the judge's head. 'You have been found guilty of three terrible murders. Having regard to the state of the law at the moment I don't propose to pass any sentence on the first or second counts. If I had, it would have been life imprisonment. But as the law stands, now that you have been found guilty of two murders on different occasions in Great Britain, the only sentence I am permitted to pass on you is that you suffer death in the manner prescribed by law, and may the Lord have mercy on your soul.'

Copeland stood impassive. Then he turned briskly on his heels, still expressionless, and was hurried out of the dock into the cells below. There, it is believed, he sat stunned and even his lawyers were advised not to try to see him as he was in shock. Upstairs, the judge thanked the jury for their service and said their grim task was now over.

And so, one of Britain's biggest and most historic criminal investigations had come to an end. Five years, around 100,000 statements taken, the finger of suspicion aimed at many men, and a bill to local ratepayers running into many thousands of pounds. At last, Chesterfield, embroiled in scandal and notoriety for so long, could begin its journey back to normality and respectability. Copeland was on his way to the gallows. But was he? Like many aspects of this remarkable case, the story didn't end there.

PART SIX

THE AFTERMATH

41

Michael Copeland didn't appeal. And he didn't hang.

The Government of the day were in the process of abolishing capital punishment and he was reprieved, the Home Secretary Sir Frank Soskice reducing the sentence to life imprisonment.

It was the beginning of the end of mandatory death sentences dating back to early Anglo-Saxon times. In days gone by, he might have been taken to purpose-built gallows by horse and cart, hung from a tree, or dragged to a public place and hanged before a rowdy crowd. But by the 1950s, after a couple of high-profile executions of people who were later found to be innocent, the public appetite for 'a life for a life' was receding.

The last people to hang in Britain were Peter Allen and Gwynne Evans who'd been convicted of killing a driver during the act of robbing him in Cumbria. They went to the gallows in August 1964 - just eight months before Copeland was found guilty. It meant that those long prosecution delays in charging him that he'd complained of so bitterly had almost certainly saved his life!

But what of the case itself? Legal commentator and High Court judge Louis Blom-Cooper felt that the fact that Copeland was unlikely to hang because of the impending legislation robbed the trial of its intrinsic quality - a showpiece for a morbid public. 'What struck me most was the absence of high drama. It has been pitched on a much lower key than murder trials in the past. Where the death penalty is a fate that may befall an accused man, the trial, conviction, and execution of the killer is regarded by the community as of such magnitude that the whole criminal process assumes a public interest of monolithic proportions.'

He speculated whether Copeland, with his psychiatric issues, could have successfully pleaded to diminished responsibility. 'Under our system an accused is entitled to withhold the evidence of his mental state from the court, although paradoxically Copeland's state of mind was alluded to by the defence for the purpose of explaining how he came under the constant police surveillance and suspicion which led to him confessing "in order to clear his name."

'Yet he asked the jury to say that he did not commit any of the murders. It may be technically possible to say "I didn't do it... but if

I did, I was not mentally responsible." But if you hope to persuade a jury of your innocence, this alternative form of pleading is not a very attractive way about convincing 12 good men and true.'

There were other issues arising from the trial too, not least the treatment of homosexuals by police and society. Two men had been brutally murdered because of their sexuality. Being in love or having sex with the wrong person could make you a criminal. Smiling in the park could lead to an arrest and being in the wrong address book could cost you a prison sentence. Homosexual men were being picked up by zealous police wanting easy convictions, often for doing nothing more than looking a bit gay.

Soon after the Copeland case, several cross-party politicians sponsored a Sexual Offences Bill, a Private Member's bill which drew heavily upon the findings of the Wolfenden report and its recommendations to decriminalise homosexual activity between adults. The sponsors were Humphry Berkeley, a gay Conservative MP, Leo Abse, a shrewd Labour politician, and Lord Arran, a Tory peer. Dissent could be summed up by the Earl of Dudley who stated that homosexuals 'are the most disgusting people in the world.' Prison was too good for them - in fact that was the place where many liked to go, 'for obvious reasons.'

However, a poll commissioned by the Daily Mail found that 63% of respondents didn't believe that homosexuality should be a crime, while only 36% agreed it should, even though 93% agreed that homosexuals were 'in need of medical or psychiatric treatment.' Crucially, a majority of MPs were sympathetic to a change. The Bill's passage through Parliament was interrupted by a General Election in 1966 but the new Labour Government under Harold Wilson, promising a wave of liberal social reforms - in divorce, abortion and theatre censorship - supported it. Bob Dylan had sung that The Times They Are a-Changin'. Indeed they were.

At 5.50am on July 5th 1967 - 13 years after the Wolfenden Committee was set up - a bill to legalise homosexuality limped through its final stages in a bleary-eyed House of Commons by a single vote.

The Sexual Offences Act legalised homosexual acts in England and Wales for the first time ever. But not unconditionally. They had to be consensual, in private, and between men over 21. The law did not apply to the Armed Forces, nor to Scotland and Northern Ireland. And it did not delete the offences of buggery and gross indecency. Nevertheless, the Bill's sponsors hailed it as an 'historic milestone' and appealed to homosexuals to show their thanks by comporting themselves quietly and with dignity. 'Any form of ostentatious behaviour or any form of public flaunting would be utterly distasteful and make the sponsors regret that they had done what they had done.' The permissive society had arrived… up to a point. It didn't come close to equalising the legal status of heterosexuals and homosexuals (that would take another 38 years) and it didn't stop the arrests: between 1967 and 2003, 30,000 gay and bisexual men were convicted for behaviour that would not have been a crime had their partner been a woman.

***

Another talking point was the police tactics of tailing Copeland until he cracked and even befriending him. Detectives would take him on the town for drinks and play dominoes and cards. Many years on, a contributor to an online discussion forum, Stephen Baines, would report that his uncle and aunt kept The Crown and Cushion in Chesterfield. 'Michael Copeland used to frequent it. Detectives used to play dominoes with him in there…'

Chief Inspector Ernest Bradshaw, the main officer involved in the investigation, agreed in the trial that a 'somewhat unusual' relationship had developed between him and the accused. He became Copeland's 'guide, philosopher and friend,' ferrying him around, lending him money on at least three occasions, even trying to get him a job. This, remember, was a suspect whom in their heart of hearts detectives knew had brutally murdered three people.

In retirement, Bradshaw wrote about the case in a policing journal. On his relationship with Copeland he explained, 'My feelings were genuine and remained so - I had no intention of either deceiving him or inducing him to make a confession. However, it would equally be true to say that at this time I did not visualise to what extent I would become involved with him. Our relationship developed to such a degree that Copeland would telephone and discuss with me his possible future plans both for work and for his private life. He did obtain work and although he was somewhat erratic in this connection and regularly changed his employment, there is not the slightest doubt that he came to regard me as a friend. On one occasion, he wished to change from lodgings to some furnished rooms and I loaned him the money to do so. There were other loans and even gifts of money to him when he was particularly low in spirit. He would call at the Police Station to see me and I found that we could converse without difficulty on a number of subjects. We discussed his friendship with me and feelings for Marie and his hopes for their future together.'

Discussing Bradshaw's evidence, Mr Justice Ashworth had addressed the jury direct. 'The phrase has been used that he had become something of a father figure to Copeland. Maybe you will believe it - loans of money, gifts of money, efforts to seek work for him. Members of the jury, do these actions strike you as the actions of a man who at least has some measure of human kindness beneath his uniform?

'And if they do, do you think that Mr Bradshaw was the type of man, distinct from most police officers, to whom a desperate conscience-stricken murderer might go for help?'

Bradshaw rose to the rank of Det Chief Supt, was head of Derbyshire CID, and awarded the MBE for his services to policing. He retired in 1972 after 37 years, investigating around 20 murders, numerous attempted murders and even Britain's first kidnapping in which a ransom was demanded. He died in 2005 at the age of 92. His sons both followed in their father's footsteps and joined the Derbyshire Force.

***

There is no doubt that as well as being a ruthless killer, Copeland could also display charm. He not only befriended cops and numerous girls, but also members of the press, both nationally and locally. Journalist John Raine was a reporter covering the story, first for a freelance agency, then for Sheffield Newspapers (The Morning Telegraph and the Sheffield Star.) He told this author, 'I interviewed him at his father's house during the investigation and proclaiming his innocence. He came to my office on one occasion in Chesterfield. I well remember visiting him at his home after he had returned from Germany after the second murder. He pulled down his trousers to reveal a long scar which he said had been the result of a knife wound, defending himself against an attacker.'

Gaining access to official records relating to Michael Copeland has been problematic: however, a trawl through public records of births, deaths and marriages reveals an interesting development that none of the families involved knew about. On the 10th July 1991 at Rutland Register Office, Michael Copeland married Margaret Aileen McLernon, a divorced nurse, whose address was given as Castle Road in Maidstone, Kent. They were both 53 years old. His address was given as 206 Ashwell Road, Oakham, Leicestershire and his profession given as a driver. It follows therefore that he must have been released from prison some time before then, having served around 25 years inside. It is not known in what circumstances he met his bride. However, something must have gone wrong with his rehabilitation because he was later back inside.

An anonymous prisoner posted online that he'd spent time in prison with Copeland long after he got married. 'I can confirm that he was still alive when I left in mid 2011. He was in bad health. He was released in the early 2000s but recalled after a matter of months as he simply could not adjust to life outside as everything as he knew it had changed. He attempted suicide and was recalled for his and everyone's safety. I spent almost two years on the same wing as him and always collected his milk and breakfast for him every morning.

'He never spoke much about the murders, just a little detail here and there. He said they were called the "bubble car murders" which meant nothing to me then as I was much younger. He was a very talented artist and I tried to purchase some of his work which he refused to sell, even for £1,000. I was told at a later date from Michael's closest friend in there that these were of the moorland where the murders were committed.

'I am glad that I had the chance to meet this man as he was a very interesting individual who I would spend up to four hours a day chatting to. That may sound weird to a lot of people but he was a very nice man and very polite. Fifty years on from the crimes, age had obviously taken its toll so of course he was no threat to me. I can honestly say that meeting this man, hearing his wisdom and stories of prison life changed me for the better and I haven't offended at all since. The last I knew he went to HMP Sudbury in Derbyshire preparing for release again.'

Without access to official records, the circumstances of Copeland's years inside - his release, mental state, marriage, and reasons for his readmission - we can only speculate upon. We do know, however, that he died in hospital of natural causes in 2013 while back in Sudbury prison.

42

Copeland's murder spree naturally holds painful memories for the surviving families of the victims.

***

In the small market town of Verden, Germany, the grieving mother of 16-year-old Guenther Helmbrecht posed for photographs clutching a framed photograph of her dead son. She also lost her husband soon afterwards.

Guenther's mother

William Elliott, who was a bachelor, has no surviving relatives. He lived with his two sisters who passed away shortly after Copeland was sentenced. He rests where he grew up - in Derbyshire, in the family grave at St Giles' Church, Great Longstone.

The Elliott family grave

***

After her husband's murder, George Stobbs' widow Josephine returned to London where she would spend the rest of her life. She never discussed his death, nor the full truth, not even to her sons later in adult life. They grew up believing their dad had died after being hit over the head by a hitchhiker. Her late husband's family gradually cut her off and she took up work as a teacher, never remarrying. She died in 2002 aged 89 having been cared for by her loving family and her sons.

Jerry Stobbs, a retired accountant now in his mid-seventies, was 12-years-old and away at boarding school when his father was killed. His cousins collected him and his brother from school and they stayed with relatives for a while. 'We were never told the details. I remember being shielded from the television news because the killing was quite a big story,' says Jerry.

'It is difficult to put the record straight regarding my father when we don't know how he is being portrayed, although the standards of the time viewed homosexuality in a different and intolerant way compared to today, so I imagine he is not portrayed in a favourable light. However, to my brother and I he was a loving father with a strong sense of humour and that is how we remember him.

'He was into jazz and had a number of 78 records, including Duke Ellington and Red Nicholls and the Five Pennies. In the 1950s we didn't have a television - few people did - so we would often listen to the radio in the evening with him, tuning into the American Forces Radio Network that played jazz and early rock and roll.

'We played cards with our parents, particularly Canasta, and followed the adventures of Dick Barton: Secret Agent on the radio. He was keen on fishing and used to take us with him, although I was far more interested in kicking a football along the water's edge. He used to have The Daily Express delivered and he once quoted from an article he was reading, "Do you know, you stand more chance of being murdered than you do of winning the Football Pools." He never did win the Pools!

'When my father died my mother was left high and dry. No pension, or other income, and living in a rented house with two boys to bring up. She got a lot of support from her family and worked as a teacher at a private school in Wimbledon to be near relatives.'

Extraordinarily, it was his father, reaching out from beyond the grave, that finally led them to the truth. Jerry has four daughters, one of whom, Georgina, is named after both her grandfathers, who were both called George, and both dogged by tragedy. Grandad George on her mother's side committed suicide and Grandad George on her father's side was murdered. She explains, 'Throughout childhood I always yearned for a grandfather. They both passed before we were born and us girls all felt we'd missed out. We'd always believed that Grandad Stobbs had been killed while giving someone a lift.

'On reflection, I'm sure this correlates with my lifelong interest in genealogy, psychology and criminology.' Indeed, her favourite TV programme was Cracker, the police drama about a criminal psychologist.

After being brought up in West Sussex, Georgina won a place at Birmingham University to study for a degree in Psychology. As part of her course, she had to write an essay in the Child Development module. This got her thinking about her own childhood and her murdered grandfather. It was around this time she began to suffer anxiety and panic attacks. And then Grandad Stobbs visited her in her dreams. 'I had a series of very vivid dreams in which we spoke to each other, we held hands, and he urged me to discover the truth,' she says. She spent hours in Birmingham Central Library looking up old newspaper archives, without luck. Then she had to write an essay about the child development of serial killers.

'My then brother-in-law was a police officer and had many books about serial killers, including one which me and my younger sister bought for him. He brought them to our house to help me with the research. One evening, sitting on the bedroom floor, looking for information by chance we stumbled on a chapter about our grandfather. The truth - and the full horror - dawned. We were all hysterical. It was a huge shock.'

The whole Copeland story is one of repeating coincidences. They realised later that the date on the day they found out that shocking truth was March 28 2001 - forty years to the day that their grandfather was murdered. The girls then had the delicate task of informing their father that his dad was killed not by a hitchhiker, but after going on a homosexual rendezvous. They approached Mum first for advice - and then gently told their dad one night. 'He'd boxed away a lot of his grief but he accepted it.'

Jerry says, 'They showed me the article. It was a shock. I tend to lock bad things away and not deal them.'

With the awful truth known to his family, George Gerald Stobbs could at last rest in peace - but not before saying a final goodbye to his granddaughter.

'I had one more dream when we were together. I told him that I now knew all about his death. We hugged and said goodbye.' Later, she wrote a poem about the whole experience called **The Visitor**.

The first time,
Opaque, frozen,
A wall of ice stands between us,
A shadowy figure moves on the other side,
I should be afraid, but warmth envelops me.

The second time,
Frosted glass, slowly thawing,
I'm relieved to be here again,
The face, distorted behind the icy barrier,
Oddly familiar, realisation washes over me.
The third time.
Clear, transparent,
A thin sheet of glass stands between us,

His hand reaches out, palm to palm,
I look into his eyes, I've seen them before,
On another face, in another time.

The fourth time.
He is other worldly, finally free,
As we hold each other, I feel our connection,
Stretching across time and space,
He has always been here watching over us.

The fifth time.
Excited to be in his presence,
We talk for hours upon hours,
Of life and tribulations, of adventures and dreams,
Advice and guidance, he helps me on my path .

The sixth time,
My hands held in his,
Blessed to be in his presence, we talk some more,
A life snatched away too soon, generations
Living with a hole left by his absence.

The last time,
I know we won't meet again,
The truth, revealed through his counsel,
To questions left unanswered for decades,
As tears drown us, we say goodbye, a tight embrace.

So off he went,
His soul to the other land,
Never to visit the dreamscape again,
Now we know the reason he was taken too soon,
We are all able to rest in peace.

That all happened when she was 20. Now, aged 42, with a family of her own, and holding down a job with the NHS as a psychological Wellbeing Practitioner, her anxiety issues have reduced significantly. And her grandad has never returned.

George Stobbs

-43-

Epilogue

How much does the public have a right to know about crimes from the past and the mental make-up of people who kill? Surely we can protect ourselves better by studying the behaviour patterns of convicted murderers?

Shortly after publication of my true crime book Pottery Cottage, I was contacted by Angela Fry, the widow of the former Sheffield journalist Tony Fry. She'd been clearing out her attic and stumbled upon Tony's cuttings from his days as a reporter and Assistant Editor on the Sheffield Morning Telegraph. The collection included his reports of a murder trial in the 1960s called the Bubble Car Murder. Would I be interested in using them as a basis for a book?

To be honest, despite living in the area for many years, I'd never heard of the Bubble Car Murder, nor for that matter, the Copy Cat Killings. Out of politeness more than anything, I called round and collected a cardboard box. Inside, threadbare and yellowed, were clippings of his reports from the trial in Birmingham dating back more than 60 years - plus his immaculate (but for me indecipherable) Pitman shorthand notes, along with his orange notebook of dates and address etc. They were indeed a fascinating read, but of course I needed much, much more research to ever write a book about the case. There is, of course, no such thing as the absolute truth - just ask sports fans who'll invariably have different versions of the same incident or event, or a police officer interviewing witnesses to a crime. There is, however, an official truth - as seen through the eyes of law enforcement. Even then, it is partial. Evidence is gathered not in search of a comprehensive set of facts, but to satisfy the demands of justice.

My first step was to approach Derbyshire Police for access to the case files under the Freedom of Information Act. This was the Force's biggest investigation ever, a landmark event, of huge public and historical interest. I assumed getting information would be straightforward. A similar request during research for Pottery Cottage resulted in a senior officer coming to my home with several boxes of witness statements, operational reports and background on Billy Hughes, who murdered four members of a family in a Peak District cottage. The bullet recovered from his head during the post mortem rolled across my kitchen table and fell on the floor!

However, this time I began to hit snags. The files were off site in storage and would need to be tracked down and indexed which would take several weeks. Fair enough. Then the Covid pandemic struck. The subsequent lockdowns delayed the process further and the weeks of waiting became months. When restrictions eased, I chased the Force's Freedom of Information Officer who admitted he'd forgotten all about the application but would get back to me as soon as possible. Then a bombshell dropped. As part of his due diligence, he'd discovered a note in the official files housed in The National Archive at Kew. In January 1996, someone from the Crown Prosecution Service had decided to seal the records from public view until - wait for it - the year 2050: 90 years after the crimes! We both thought it must be a mistake. However, he could not decide on my application while the note was active, so in September 2021 I duly applied under the Freedom of Information Act to the National Archive for access. Eight months later I was informed that the information would remain withheld from the public. The Crown Prosecution Service decided that disclosure would be likely to endanger the mental health of the victims' families including those of Michael Copeland himself. It also ruled that under Data Protection laws it would be unfair and might cause distress to a number of other individuals involved in the case.

I requested a review of the decision, arguing there was huge public interest in making the files available to the public, not just for authors like me, but for society as a whole, including of course the victims' families. I contended they had a right to know the full circumstances of the crimes, particularly the make-up and background of the serial killer who murdered their dad.

Parliament's intention by voting in the Freedom of Information Act was clear - that in a free, democratic society openness was paramount. Virtually all of the detail was already in the public domain anyhow. The court case, including distressing evidence on how the victims met their deaths, was widely reported at the time, and Det Supt Ernest Bradshaw, the main officer involved, had written a lengthy and detailed report on the investigation for a police journal now easily accessible on the internet. Scene of crime photos were also published online.

The notion that publication would risk damaging the mental health of the victims' families is laughable. William Elliott's only remaining family - his sisters - died half a century ago; the family of Guenther Helmbrecht know all the horrific details of his murder and came to England twice to give evidence, even posing for photographs; George Stobbs' widow died in 2012, and the couple's sons, now in their mid-70s, know the full details of their father's homosexuality, and are happy that the full truth be known. Indeed, they were happy to contribute to my book with words and pictures.

However, the manager of the Freedom of Information Centre at the National Archives, whilst conceding the deliberation took an unreasonable amount of time (153 working days), upheld the CPS decision.

The ruling said, 'disclosure of the distressing content held within the file would place in the public domain detailed and intimate accounts of traumatic events, which would force these individuals and their families to confront this information in inappropriate circumstances. I note that you are already aware of existing information surrounding the case which is already available in the public domain. While I recognise the release of this file could add to the historical account of this case, this does not outweigh the public interest in protecting the rights and freedoms of individuals identified within the file.'

That includes Michael Copeland, a convicted killer, who has cost taxpayers and ratepayers hundreds of thousands of pounds to treat and care for in prison.

The decision was not binding on Derbyshire Police and in the summer of 2022, I renewed my FOI request to them. I sought access to the dead killer's medical and psychiatric files now hidden from the public for another 30 years. They too took the CPS line, even refusing my request to discuss the case with a senior officer. As mentioned previously, we can only speculate on Copeland's years inside - his mental state and the reasons for his readmission - in the absence of information from official records.

As the famous law expert Louis Blom-Cooper wrote the day after the trial, 'Thus, once again, our criminal process - impeccably fair to the accused - has revealed to the public less than the truth about the crime and the person who committed it. If we are to prevent murders, we must learn more about the factors that produce the homicidal situation. What makes men kill? At least the consignment of the hangman's noose to the museum will preserve the lives of killers whom we can then study. Perhaps we shall then learn about man's propensities to kill.' Wishful thinking, Louis. However, I have submitted a fresh Freedom of Information request to the National Archive for access to Copeland's prison records which was still under consideration as this book was published.

***

Perhaps the last word should go the family of George Gerard Stobbs, still grieving at his loss more than 60 years on.

George's grandaughter Georgina is saddened at how he had to lead a secret life as a closet homosexual. 'It must have been awful for him,' she said. None of the family would feel mentally harmed by the National Archive records being released.

'I wonder why the records are sealed when internet sites contain so much information on the murders anyway. Indeed, I found photos of grandad's body in situ where it had been found.

'Copeland was friends with a Chief Inspector in the police force and the cynic in me believes this has more to do with it?'

Georgina and her sisters must wait until they are in their seventies - 2050 - for the official truth to be known. By then, George's sons Jerry and Nicholas will most likely have passed away themselves. Jerry never knew about Copeland's release from prison and marriage but says that this book has helped him - at the age of 75 - to finally come to terms with the full detail of his father's murder.

A MESSAGE FROM THE AUTHOR

Before you go…

Thank you for purchasing my book. I hope you enjoyed it. Can I ask a small favour? Would you be kind enough to post a review on Amazon? Good, bad, or indifferent, one or five stars, it doesn't matter. Online reviews are so important for independent publishers like myself. They trigger the algorithms, and help bring the book to the attention of new readers. Just go on the Amazon website and type in the book title. Just a few lines make all the difference.

Thank you for your support.

ALAN HURNDALL

Printed in Great Britain
by Amazon